# AI and the Future of Creative Work

This book focuses on the intelligent technologies that are transforming creative practices and industries.

The future of creative work will be more complicated than "the robots will take our jobs." The workplace is becoming increasingly hybridized, with human and computational labor complementing each other. Some economic roles for the former will no doubt fade over time, while new roles are created to produce artificial intelligence (AI)-related technologies and implementations for productivity. New tools for the generation and personalization of content across platforms will be as ubiquitous as the automation of repetitive tasks in content creation workflows. Cultural conceptions of what it means to be a creative worker will necessarily change as a result of these transformations in human-machine labor. The volume covers the possibilities of humans and robots developing collegial relationships, creative cybernetics as machines and artists become co-creators of art, the reconcentration of corporate power as AI transforms the music industry, the rhetoric of algorithm-driven cultural production in streaming media and how artisans provide a model of counter-hegemony to automation processes.

Scholars and students from many backgrounds, as well as policy makers, journalists and the general reading public, will find a multidisciplinary approach to questions posed by creative labor and industry research from communication, philosophy, robotics, media, music and the creative arts, informatics, information science, and computer science and engineering.

**Michael Filimowicz** is Senior Lecturer in the School of Interactive Arts and Technology (SIAT) at Simon Fraser University. He has a background in computer-mediated communications, audiovisual production, new media art and creative writing. His research develops new multimodal display technologies and forms, exploring novel form factors across different application contexts including gaming, immersive exhibitions and simulations.

**Algorithms and Society**

Series Editor

Dr Michael Filimowicz

*Senior Lecturer in the School of Interactive Arts and Technology (SIAT) at Simon Fraser University.*

As algorithms and data flows increasingly penetrate every aspect of our lives, it is imperative to develop sufficient theoretical lenses and design approaches to humanize our informatic devices and environments. At stake are the human dimensions of society which stand to lose ground to calculative efficiencies and performance, whether at the service of government, capital, criminal networks, or even a general mob concatenated in social media.

Algorithms and Society is a new series which takes a broad view of the information age. Each volume focuses on an important thematic area, from new fields such as software studies and critical code studies to more established areas of inquiry such as philosophy of technology and science and technology studies. This series aims to stay abreast of new areas of controversy and social issues as they emerge with the development of new technologies.

If you wish to submit a book proposal for the series, please contact Dr Michael Filimowicz michael_f@sfu.ca or Emily Briggs emily.briggs@tandf.co.uk

**AI and the Future of Creative Work**
Algorithms and Society
*Edited by Michael Filimowicz*

**China's Digital Civilization**
Algorithms and Society
*Edited by Michael Filimowicz*

**Decolonizing Data**
Algorithms and Society
*Edited by Michael Filimowicz*

**Information Disorder**
Algorithms and Society
*Edited by Michael Filimowicz*

For more information on the series, visit: www.routledge.com/Algorithms-and-Society/book-series/ALGRAS

# AI and the Future of Creative Work

## Algorithms and Society

**Edited by Michael Filimowicz**

LONDON AND NEW YORK

First published 2023
by Routledge
4 Park Square, Milton Park, Abingdon, Oxon OX14 4RN

and by Routledge
605 Third Avenue, New York, NY 10158

*Routledge is an imprint of the Taylor & Francis Group, an informa business*



*British Library Cataloguing-in-Publication Data*
A catalogue record for this book is available from the British Library

*Library of Congress Cataloging-in-Publication Data*
Names: Filimowicz, Michael, editor.
Title: AI and the future of creative work: algorithms and society/edited by Michael Filimowicz.
Description: Abingdon, Oxon; New York, NY: Routledge, 2023. | Series: Algorithms and society | Includes bibliographical references and index.
Identifiers: LCCN 2023009403 (print) | LCCN 2023009404 (ebook) | ISBN 9781032290638 (hardback) | ISBN 9781032290645 (paperback) | ISBN 9781003299875 (ebook)
Subjects: LCSH: Cultural industries—Technological innovations. | Artificial intelligence—Industrial applications. | Arts—Economic aspects.
Classification: LCC HD9999.C9472 A42 2024 (print) | LCC HD9999.C9472 (ebook) | DDC 331.7/617—dc23/eng/20230302
LC record available at https://lccn.loc.gov/2023009403
LC ebook record available at https://lccn.loc.gov/2023009404

ISBN: 978-1-032-29063-8 (hbk)
ISBN: 978-1-032-29064-5 (pbk)
ISBN: 978-1-003-29987-5 (ebk)

DOI: 10.4324/9781003299875

Typeset in Times New Roman
by Apex CoVantage, LLC

# Contents

*List of Figures* *vi*
*Notes on Contributors* *vii*
*Series Preface* *x*
*Volume Introduction* *xiii*

1 **Can a Robot Be a (Good) Colleague?** 1
SVEN NYHOLM

2 **Creative Machine-Human Collaboration: Toward a Cybernetic Approach to Artificial Intelligence and Machine Learning Techniques in the Creative Arts** 18
STEPHEN RODDY

3 **Slave to the 'Rithm: The AI Turn in the Music Industries** 36
SARAH KEITH, STEVE COLLINS, ADRIAN RENZO AND ALEX MESKER

4 **A "New Economy" of Blockbusters?: Netflix, Algorithms and the Narratives of Transformation in Audiovisual Capitalism** 55
CHRISTOPHE MAGIS

5 **Counter-hegemonic AI: The Role of Artisanal Identity in the Design of Automation for a Liberated Economy** 71
MATTHEW GARVIN, RON EGLASH, KWAME PORTER ROBINSON, LIONEL ROBERT, MARK GUZDIAL AND AUDREY BENNETT

*Index* *89*

# Figures


| | | |
|---|---|---|
| 4.1 | Netflix's content spending (worldwide, in billion US dollars) | 64 |
| 4.2 | Netflix's content assets, by type (worldwide, in billion US dollars) | 64 |
| 4.3 | Netflix's paid subscribers (worldwide, in millions) | 67 |

# Contributors

**Professor Audrey Bennett** is a design scholar of Afro-Caribbean descent, an inaugural University Diversity and Social Transformation Professor of the University of Michigan, and Professor of Art and Design at U-M's Penny W. Stamps School of Art and Design.

**Steve Collins** is Senior Lecturer in Multimedia in the Department of Media, Communications, Creative Arts, Language and Literature at Macquarie University, Sydney, Australia. His research focuses on copyright law, musical creativity, digital technologies and disruption in the creative industries. He is the coauthor of *Beyond 2.0: The Future of Music* (Equinox, 2014).

**Ron Eglash** is Professor in the School of Information at the University of Michigan, with a secondary appointment in the School of Art and Design. He received his B.S. in cybernetics, his M.S. in systems engineering and his Ph.D. in history of consciousness, all from the University of California. His work includes *African Fractals: Modern Computing and Indigenous Design* (1999) and *Appropriating Technology: Vernacular Science and Social Power* (1994). His *Culturally Situated Design Tools* (csdt.org), online applications for ethnocomputing and Generative Justice (https://generative justice.org), a website for decolonial circular economies, are funded by the National Science Foundation.

**Matthew Garvin** is a Ph.D. student in the School of Information at the University of Michigan, where he also earned his M.S. Prior to this, he received his B.A. in anthropology from Wayne State University. His research explores the intersections of design, technology and the future of work on Earth and in space.

**Mark Guzdial** is Professor in Computer Science and Engineering and Director of the Program in Computing in the Arts and Sciences at the University of Michigan. He studies how people learn computing and how to improve that learning. He was one of the founders of the International Computing Education Research conference. He is an ACM Distinguished Educator and a Fellow of the ACM.

**Sarah Keith** is Lecturer in Music and Media in the Department of Media, Communications, Creative Arts, Language and Literature at Macquarie University, Sydney, Australia. Her research focuses on popular music and culture, particularly in the Australian and East Asian context, as well as music technology, and music and screen.

**Christophe Magis** is Associate Professor of Political Economy of Communications at Université Paris 8 (France), where he is also Director of the Master Program in Music Business Management. His research interests include the critical political economy of cultural and communication industries and the epistemology of critical theories in communication. He is currently working on the rise of the recording business in the history of the culture industry.

**Alex Mesker** is Associate Lecturer in Music in the Department of Media, Communications, Creative Arts, Language and Literature at Macquarie University, Sydney, Australia. His research focuses on the use of soundtrack libraries in television animation, film soundtrack studies, music information retrieval and computational arts.

**Sven Nyholm** is Professor of the Ethics of Artificial Intelligence at the Ludwig Maximilian University of Munich in Germany. Nyholm's research focuses on issues within the ethics of technology—particularly the ethics of artificial intelligence and robotics—as well as on ethical theory more generally. His publications include the books *Revisiting Kant's Universal Law and Humanity Formulas* (De Gruyter 2015), *Humans and Robots: Ethics, Agency, and Anthropomorphism* (Rowman & Littlefield International 2020) and *This Is Technology Ethics: An Introduction* (Wiley-Blackwell 2023).

**Adrian Renzo** is Lecturer in Music in the Department of Media, Communications, Creative Arts, Language and Literature at Macquarie University, Sydney, Australia. His research explores how sample-based music is assembled, how popular music fans negotiate hierarchies of taste and how electronic dance music intersects with Top 40 pop.

**Dr. Lionel Robert** is Professor in the School of Information and core faculty in the Robotics Institute at the University of Michigan as well as an AIS Distinguished Member Cum Laude and an IEEE Senior Member. He completed his Ph.D. in information systems from Indiana University, where he was a BAT Fellow and KPMG Scholar. He is also the director of the Michigan Autonomous Vehicle Research Intergroup Collaboration (MAVRIC), an affiliate of the National Center for Institutional Diversity and Indiana University's Center for Computer-Mediated Communication.

**Kwame Porter Robinson** is a Ph.D. candidate in the School of Information at the University of Michigan. He received his master's in computer science from the University of Maryland, Baltimore County; a B.F.A. in graphic design from Boston University; and a B.S. in electrical engineering from New Mexico State University. Kwame investigates how people can flourish through community-defined economic systems. His topics of study include generative justice and using artificial intelligence with communities to define and refine economic systems.

**Stephen Roddy** is an artist and researcher and lecturer working at the intersection of technology and the creative arts. He holds a Ph.D. in sonification, the use of sound to perceptualize data, from Trinity College Dublin, where he is currently an assistant professor in the Department of Film.

# Series Preface

## Algorithms and Society

*Michael Filimowicz*

This series is less about what algorithms are and more about how they act in the world through "eventful" (Bucher, 2018, p. 48) forms of "automated decision making" (Noble, 2018, loc. 141) in which computational models are "based on choices made by fallible human beings" (O'Neil, 2016, loc. 126).

> Decisions that used to be based on human refection are now made automatically. Software encodes thousands of rules and instructions computed in a fraction of a second.
>
> (Pasquale, 2015, loc. 189)

> If, in the industrial era, the promise of automation was to displace manual labor, in the information age it is to pre-empt agency, spontaneity, and risk: to map out possible futures before they hap-pen so objectionable ones can be foreclosed and desirable ones selected.
>
> (Andrejevic, 2020, p. 8)

> [M]achine learning algorithms that anticipate our future propensities are seriously threatening the chances that we have to make possible alternative political futures.
>
> (Amoore, 2020, p. xi)

Algorithms, definable pragmatically as "a method for solving a problem" (Finn, 2017, loc. 408), "leap from one feld to the next" (O'Neil, 2016, loc. 525). They are "hyperobjects: things with such broad temporal and spatial reach that they exceed the phenomenological horizon of human subjects" (Hong, 2020, p. 30). While in the main, the techno-logical systems taken up as volume topics are design solutions to problems for which there are commercial markets, organized communities, or claims of state interest, their power and ubiquity generate new problems for inquiry. The series will do its part to track this domain fuidity across its volumes and contest, through critique and investigation, their "logic of secrecy" (Pasquale, 2015, loc. 68), and "obfuscation" (loc. 144).

These new social (rather than strictly computational) problems that are generated can, in turn, be taken up by many critical, policy, and speculative discourses. At their most productive, such debates can potentially alter the ethical, legal, and even imaginative parameters of the environments in which the algorithms of our information architectures and infrastructures operate, as algorithmic implementations often reflect a "desire for epistemic purity, of knowledge stripped of uncertainty and human guesswork" (Hong, 2020, p. 20). The series aims to foster a general intervention in the conversation around these often "black boxed" technologies and track their pervasive effects in society.

> Contemporary algorithms are not so much transgressing settled societal norms as establishing new patterns of good and bad, new thresholds of normality and abnormality, against which actions are calibrated.
>
> (Amoore, 2020, p. 5)

Less "hot button" algorithmic topics are also of interest to the series, such as their use in the civil sphere by citizen scientists, activists, and hobbyists, where there is usually not as much discursive attention. Beyond private, state, and civil interests, the increasingly sophisticated technology-based activities of criminals, whether amateur or highly organized, deserve broader attention as now everyone must defend their digital identities. The information systems of companies and states conduct a general form of "ambient surveillance" (Pasquale, 2015, loc. 310), and anyone can be a target of a hacking operation.

Algorithms and Society thus aims to be an interdisciplinary series which is open to researchers from a broad range of academic back-grounds. While each volume has its defined scope, chapter contributions may come from many areas such as sociology, communications, critical legal studies, criminology, digital humanities, economics, computer science, geography, computational media and design, philosophy of technology, and anthropology, along with others. Algorithms are "shaping the conditions of everyday life" (Bucher, 2018, p. 158) and operate "at the intersection of computational space, cultural systems, and human cognition" (Finn, 2017, loc. 160), so the multidisciplinary terrain is vast indeed. Since the series is based on the shorter Routledge Focus format, it can be nimble and responsive to emerging areas of debate in fast-changing technological domains and their sociocultural impacts.

## References

Amoore, L. (2020). *Cloud ethics: Algorithms and the attributes of ourselves and others*. Duke University Press.

Andrejevic, M. (2020). *Automated media*. Taylor and Francis.
Bucher, T. (2018). *If... then: Algorithmic power and politics*. Oxford University Press.
Finn, E. (2017). *What algorithms want: Imagination in the age of computing* [Kindle Version]. MIT Press.
Hong, S. H. (2020). *Technologies of speculation: The limits of knowledge in a data-driven society*. New York University Press.
Noble, S. U. (2018). *Algorithms of oppression* [Kindle Version]. New York University Press.
O'Neil, C. (2016). *Weapons of math destruction* [Kindle Version]. Broadway Books.
Pasquale, F. (2015). *The black box society* [Kindle Version]. Harvard University Press.

# Volume Introduction

The future of creative work will be more complicated than "the robots will take our jobs." The workplace is becoming increasingly hybridized with human and computational labor complementing each other. Some economic roles for the former will no doubt fade over time, while new roles are created to produce artificial intelligence (AI)-related technologies and implementations for productivity. New tools for the generation and personalization of content across platforms will be as ubiquitous as the automation of repetitive tasks in content creation workflows. Cultural conceptions of what it means to be a creative worker will necessarily change as a result of these transformations in human-machine labor.

Chapter 1—"Can a Robot Be a (Good) Colleague? " by Sven Nyholm—addresses three philosophical questions: Can a robot be a colleague? Can a robot be a good colleague? Can collegial relationships be realized between humans and robots? Those who work with robots often bond with them and consider them teammates. This chapter proposes that a robot might be a co-worker and behave like a good one according to how certain terms are defined, though workplace human-robot contact is unlikely to satisfy some qualities like worker solidarity and recognition.

Chapter 2—"Creative Machine-Human Collaboration: Toward a Cybernetic Approach to Artificial Intelligence and Machine Learning Techniques in the Creative Arts" by Stephen Roddy—discusses artificial intelligence and machine learning/deep learning applications in art making from technical and creative perspectives, focusing on two problematic topics: the master-servant dynamic and the fear that the smart machine may replace the artist users. The chapter is informed by creative cybernetics and composer George E. Lewis's ideas, whose comportment toward these tools as co-creators addresses these issues.

Chapter 3—"Slave to the 'Rithm: The AI Turn in the Music Industries" by Sarah Keith, Steve Collins, Adrian Renzo and Alex Mesker—acknowledges AI's many benefits to music makers and practitioners—such as democratizing creation and enabling low- or no-cost participation—or to businesses—such as generating higher-quality market insights. However, the "AI pivot" in the music industry also reconcentrates corporate power in a few digital intermediaries, who control finance, expertise and access. The authors focus on five emerging trends in music and AI: streaming oligopolies, music datafication, music as a digital asset, changes in the value of music artifacts and the rise of sub-amateurs who rely on centralized technologies.

Chapter 4—"A 'New Economy' of Blockbusters? Netflix, Algorithms and the Narratives of Transformation in Audiovisual Capitalism" by Christophe Magis—examines the rhetoric around Netflix and other subscription video on demand (SVOD) companies' recommendation algorithms and audiovisual production economics. This rhetoric—carried out by business actors, media commentators and even academics—sees such algorithms as key to a major media risk reduction strategy change. Netflix's socioeconomic methods illustrate that, while the idea of algorithm-driven content creation is growing, the actual strategies tend to follow well-established audiovisual industry cultural logics.

Chapter 5—"Counter-hegemonic AI: The Role of Artisanal Identity in the Design of Automation for a Liberated Economy" by Matthew Garvin, Ron Eglash, Kwame Porter Robinson, Lionel Robert, Mark Guzdial and Audrey Bennett—raises awareness of the rich history of artisans that can be a key resource for designers of a liberated economy by documenting technology-based counter-hegemonic movements and identities. Artisans provide a contemporary environment for perceiving work as a liberated form of expression based on more equitable and sustainable patterns. They provide models for participatory design, solidarity design and other methods that can transform automation processes toward fostering an unalienated economy.

Michael Filimowicz

## Acknowledgment

The chapter summaries here have in places drawn from the authors' chapter abstracts, the full versions of which can be found in Routledge's online reference for the volume.

# 1 Can a Robot Be a (Good) Colleague?

*Sven Nyholm*

The idea of robots with artificial intelligence (AI) that work for us human beings existed long before the word "robot" did. Aristotle and some other ancient Greeks imagined animated instruments—what we would now call robots—that could take over work they thought that human slaves were needed for. In one striking passage, Aristotle wrote:

> [I]f each instrument could do its own work, at the word of command or by intelligent anticipation, like the statues of Daedalus or the tripods of Hephaestus . . . a shuttle could then weave of itself, and a plectrum would do its own harp playing. In this situation, managers would not need subordinates and masters would not need slaves.
>
> (Aristotle, 1957; quoted in Devecka, 2013, pp. 54–55)

When the word "robot" was later invented—in a 1920 play called *Rossum's Universal Robots*—it was associated with the same general idea (Royakkers & van Est, 2015). The playwright Karel Čapek used the Czech language word for forced labor—"robota"—and turned it into a noun: "robot." And the robots in the play were artificial humans working in a factory.

About one hundred years later, in 2021, the technology entrepreneur Elon Musk gave a presentation in which he claimed that his car company Tesla were working on a humanoid robot: the "Tesla bot." Musk said that this real-life humanoid robot could take over boring tasks from human beings and work in Tesla factories where they would build cars for us humans. Musk further claimed that the Tesla bot would be programmed to only want to serve and be "friendly" toward human beings (Nyholm, 2023, chapter 8).

In other words, the idea of robots that work for human beings—taking over the work that human beings otherwise have to do—goes back a long time. The fantasy that those robots would be humanlike is a recurring theme both in science fiction and in real-life visions of the future. There is also the idea, however, of human beings working together with robots—a little like the robots C3PO and R2D2, which are part of a team together with human beings in the old *Star Wars* movies. In other words, in this alternative vision,

DOI: 10.4324/9781003299875-1

the robots would be working for us human beings, but they would not be able to do all the work completely on their own but would rather need to work together with human beings.

For examples of this idea, we do not need to go to musings from the ancient Greeks, science fiction or visions from tech entrepreneurs. We already have robots "working" alongside human beings in the real world—which may not resemble artificial human beings but which are nevertheless sometimes seen as members of the team by the human beings who work with these robots.

A striking example of this is documented by the technology researcher Julie Carpenter (2015) in her fascinating book *Culture and Human-Robot Interaction in Militarized Spaces: A War Story*. Carpenter interviewed American soldiers in the battlefield in Iraq, who were working with bomb disposal robots. Those robots didn't at all look like paradigmatic robots or the artificial humans in the Čapek play. They looked more like small tanks. They could not talk or act like human beings. Nevertheless, the human beings working alongside these bomb disposal robots got very attached to them and started regarding them as valued members of the team—as colleagues, if you will. This was evident when one of these robots—"Boomer"—was blown up by a bomb. The soldiers didn't want to replace the robot. They instead wanted to repair that particular robot, even if there were newer, better models available.

When Boomer was finally damaged beyond repair, the soldiers in the team wanted to give Boomer an improvised military funeral and two Medals of Honor: a Purple Heart and a Bronze Star. The soldiers said they were going to deeply miss Boomer and that "he" had "develop[ed] a personality of his own" (Garber, 2013). Remarkably, they regarded Boomer the robot as a valued member of the team and a colleague of sufficient importance to merit being honored like a fallen human comrade might have been.

This second idea of working robots—the idea of robots that work together with us and that might be regarded as members of the team—is the idea that this chapter will reflect on. Increasingly, we will be working alongside robots and other advanced technologies with AI, and some of these might come to be seen as members of the team or as colleagues by the humans who work alongside the robots. The question this chapter will discuss is whether this whole idea makes sense.

That is, while some people will regard some robots or other AI technologies as their colleagues or valued members of their teams, can a robot really be a good colleague? Or is this a case of human beings projecting human features onto technologies in a confused and potentially bad or even dangerous way? More specifically, we will consider the following three related questions:

1. Can a robot at all be a colleague, in any sense?
2. Can a robot be a good colleague, in any sense?
3. Can important values associated with collegiality be realized in the context of human-robot work teams?

The chapter will suggest that robots could be colleagues according to some definitions of what it is to be a colleague. They could perhaps even be good colleagues in a certain sense. Yet it is more doubtful whether some of the key values that we associate with good collegial relationships among human colleagues can be realized within work relationships between humans and robots. In particular, the collegial values of solidarity and recognition—which are identified as important values within collegial relationships by the philosophers Monika Betzler and Jörg Löschke (2021)—do not seem to be values it makes sense to imagine as easy or perhaps at all possible to realize within human-robot work relationships.

Here is a roadmap of what follows next. Firstly, I will say something brief about some key concepts—work, AI, robots—and comment on why it is interesting to ask the questions discussed in this chapter. Secondly, I will compare the main questions discussed in this chapter with two other questions philosophers have asked about human-robot relationships: namely whether robots can be our friends or our romantic partners. Thirdly, I will start with the question of whether a robot can be a colleague in any sensible sense. I will suggest that by certain plausible criteria, perhaps they can. Fourthly, I will discuss what I will call "performance-based" or "behavioral" criteria for being a good colleague and suggest that by such standards, it makes a certain amount of sense to think that robots can be good colleagues—at least if we understand being a good colleague as a matter of degree. Fifthly, I will consider Betzler and Löschke's ideas about values that are realized in good collegial relationships and discuss whether solidarity and recognition can be mutually realized in human-robot interaction. As noted earlier, I will suggest that we should be skeptical about this. Lastly, I will briefly discuss whether this whole discussion is somehow ethically problematic.

## Key Concepts: Work, AI, Robots

It is always a good idea to start a philosophical discussion by defining some of the key terms that will be used. Let us start with the idea of *work* in general. In this chapter, work will be understood in a somewhat narrow, economic and legalistic sense. It will be understood as a set of more or less well-defined tasks that people regularly perform, based on a contract or other agreement according to which they are financially or otherwise compensated for performing those tasks, in accordance with that contract or agreement (Danaher, 2019a). It is of course also possible to have a broader definition of "work," which would also include unpaid care work or voluntary work for which no compensation is provided. In no way does this chapter intend to suggest that work in that broader sense is less important than work in the narrower sense specified previously. However, because the topic of this chapter is the introduction of AI and robots into workplaces and the question of robots as potential colleagues, it makes sense to focus on work in the narrower sense in this context.

In this chapter, another notion of particular interest is the widely shared idea that *meaningful work* involves being part of a community or team where one has good colleagues (Smids et al., 2021). As more and more AI systems and robots are entering workplaces, the question arises of whether robots threaten our opportunities for meaningful work. Notably, many people spend much of their time at work, and they might increasingly be working alongside robots. This makes it important to reflect on whether robots could be good colleagues or whether they threaten the value related to working alongside good colleagues. Additionally, as we saw already, some people experience robots as if the robots are good colleagues. This also makes it interesting to reflect on whether such people—for example, the soldiers working alongside the bomb-disposal robot Boomer—are making some sort of mistake.

Let us next consider what we mean when we speak of AI and robots. *AI* is often understood as any form of technology that is able to perform tasks that human beings use their natural intelligence to perform (Gordon & Nyholm, 2021). Sometimes one talks about AI as *imitating* intelligent behavior or intelligent thinking, sometimes as *simulating* or *replicating* intelligent behavior or thinking (Russell & Norvig 2010). If the AI is simply operating as a computer program, the computers used are usually not labeled robots. But when there are machines with sensors and actuators, so that they can directly "perceive" and then react to their environments, the AI systems in question are usually called "robots."

A *robot*, then, is an embodied machine that is able to perform some set of tasks with the help of sensors and actuators with which they can interact with their environment in the service of their tasks (Royakkers & van Est, 2015). Any robot, therefore, can be seen as having at least a limited or narrow form of AI. That is, most robots perform tasks that can be seen as imitating, simulating or even replicating intelligent human behavior, though perhaps only in a very limited way.

Robots can look like paradigmatic robots of the sorts we associate with science fiction—for example, they might have a metallic or plastic appearance and a vaguely humanlike form. One example is the robot "Pepper." Most robots, though, have shapes and capabilities appropriate for the tasks they are intended for—which was the case with Boomer. There are, however, some robots that are designed specifically to resemble humans. One example is a small robot called "Kaspar" that was developed for use in treatment of children with autism. Another example is the well-known robot "Sophia" from Hanson Robotics (Nyholm, 2020).

Most robots that are likely to enter workplaces or that have already entered workplaces are not going to be of those humanoid types. Rather, they will typically have shapes and ways of behaving that are relevant to the work tasks they are meant to perform or take over from human beings. And yet they might potentially come to be viewed as members of the work team—just like Boomer the military robot was.

## Lessons From Philosophical Debates About Whether Robots Can Be Our Friends or Romantic Partners

The main questions discussed in this chapter have hardly been discussed within philosophical discussions about AI and robots, save for in some previous writings by the author of this chapter (Nyholm & Smids, 2020; Nyholm, 2023). In empirical research about robots in workplaces there has been some discussion about whether people can experience robots as valuable colleagues or members of their teams (e.g., Groom & Nass, 2007; Ljungblad et al., 2012; Carpenter, 2015; Sauppé & Mutlu, 2015). Here, however, we are interested in the philosophical question of whether such ways of relating to robots make sense or whether people who have such responses are making some sort of mistake. That is not something that has been discussed much yet by philosophers.

What has been discussed much more by philosophers are two other questions—namely, whether robots can be our friends or even romantic partners (e.g., Danaher, 2019b; Nyholm, 2020; Ryland, 2021). Those might seem like odd questions. But many people find them interesting. And a number of philosophers have written about them. When one approaches the topic of this chapter, one can make use of the types of arguments that have been put forward within the philosophical discussion of human-robot friendship and love. So let me briefly mention some such arguments.

In particular, two kinds of arguments are of special interest for our discussion about whether robots can be (good) colleagues. The first kind of argument investigates what kinds of behavior or performative criteria might be associated with being a good friend or a good romantic partner. The question is then whether robots could behave in the relevant ways or perform according to the relevant standards. The second kind of argument looks "within" and asks whether robots can have the right kind of attitudes, feelings or other internal states that we associate with good friends or romantic partners. The question is whether robots could have those internal states that are important for human friendship and love.

Unsurprisingly, there are more writers who think that the first kind of argument might support the possibility of human-robot friendship or love than there are writers who think that the second kind of argument might support the possibility of human-robot friendship or love. For example, the robotics researcher Maartje De Graaf (2016) and the philosopher and legal academic John Danaher (2019b) argue that when it comes to the types of behavior or the sorts of performances we associate with friendship (or perhaps even with love), it is not ruled out that robots (with advanced AI) could be made to behave like friends or romantic partners do.

This is a little bit like a so-called Turing test for personal relationships. According to the pioneering computer scientist and mathematician Alan Turing, we should not ask whether machines can think but rather whether they can behave as if they can think (Gordon & Nyholm, 2021). In the same way, Danaher argues that when we consider whether a robot can be a friend or a companion, we should ask whether they could be made to behave like a friend or companion. If so, we could consider them as our friends or companions.

That type of argument has been met with the second type of argument as a critical response. That is, some have argued that when it comes to valuable human relationships, how people behave—or some set of performative criteria—is not all that matters (Nyholm, 2020, 2023). What goes on "on the inside" matters greatly too. Whether somebody is our friend or a good romantic partner depends not only on how they behave but also on whether they have the sorts of inner attitudes, feelings or other mental states that we associate with what one can expect from a friend or a romantic partner. Otherwise, we could hire an actor to behave like a friend or a companion. It matters to us what people think, how they feel and what motivations they have. And robots cannot have the inner lives of human friends or partners. Therefore, the second type of argument can be used to argue against the possibility of human-robot friendship or love.

I bring up these arguments summarized earlier because they can be carried over to the discussion of whether robots can be good colleagues in workplaces and the distinctive values we associate with collegial relationships can be realized within human-robot interaction. But before we get to those questions, let us first consider whether it makes sense to regard robots as any kind of colleague in the first place.

## Can a Robot Be a Colleague?

To answer whether robots can be our colleagues in any sense, one needs some theory or definition of what it is for two or more individuals to be colleagues. One can then ask whether robots could play the roles that a colleague is supposed to play according to that definition or theory.

Philosophers interested in human-robot interaction have not really discussed whether a robot can be our colleagues at work. That is perhaps not very surprising, given that this would have seemed like a silly idea up until very recently. What is perhaps more surprising is that philosophers also haven't really discussed what it is for human beings to be each other's colleagues. Philosophers spend a lot of time discussing what it is to be somebody's friend or romantic partner. But the question of what it is to be somebody's colleague has not received the same attention.

However, the duo of philosophers already mentioned—Monika Betzler and Jörg Löschke (2021)—have offered a general theory of what it is for people to be colleagues. They then proceed to offer an analysis of the most important values that can be realized within such collegial relationships. We will get to that second part of their discussion later, but let's start with the first part.

In short, according to the theory that Betzler and Löschke put forward, two (or more) individuals are colleagues if at least two of the following three conditions hold.

Condition 1: the individuals have "the same work content or domain of activity."
Condition 2: the individuals have "the same institutional affiliation or common purpose."
Condition 3: the individuals have "the same status or level of responsibility" (Betzler & Löschke, 2021, p. 213).

For example, perhaps two professors at two different universities are colleagues because they have the same work content or domain of activity and because they have the same status or level of responsibility. They fulfill conditions 1 and 3. Perhaps they do not work at the same institution (though they might have a common purpose), so whether they fulfill condition 2 might be unclear. But since they fulfill two out of three conditions—which is all that the theory claims is needed—they qualify as being colleagues.

If these two imagined professors also happened to work at the same institution, they would even more clearly qualify as being colleagues, according to this theory. In other words, the theory seems to indicate that there can be degrees of collegiality. If certain individuals fulfill all three conditions, perhaps they could be said to be colleagues even more clearly or more fully than individuals who fulfill only two of the three conditions. Importantly, though, the theory only requires that two out of the three conditions hold.

What about robots? Could they be our colleagues by these criteria? Consider, as an example, robots that work alongside humans in a logistics warehouse. The humans in this warehouse and the robots might have fairly similar "work content and domain of activity": their job might be to place items in boxes and get them ready to be shipped off to people who have ordered the items. So condition 1 might be fulfilled. Consider the next condition 2. The robots and the human warehouse employees might have the "same institutional affilitation and common purpose." That is, they are part of the same company/organization, and their purpose (while at work) is to pick and pack items and to get them sent off to people who have ordered these items. So condition 2, it might be thought, is also fulfilled.

What about condition 3? Could these robots and the human employees have the same status and the same responsibilities? Here one might think that this is more doubtful. One would hope that the humans and the robots differ in their status within the organization. And it might not make sense to talk about robots as having responsibilities—unless we simply mean that the robots perform tasks similar to those the human employees have. So perhaps we should say that it is harder to imagine that the third condition would be fulfilled by robots.

However, that does not matter when it comes to deciding whether robots can be our colleagues. Only two out of the three conditions need to be fulfilled. As we just saw, the first two conditions could be fulfilled by robots—at least to some extent. So we should potentially conclude that robots could be our colleagues by the criteria that Betzler and Löschke suggest.

It might seem strange to say that a robot could be somebody's colleague—at least if we understand this to mean that a robot can be a colleague in just the same way that a human being can be a colleague. If we think of being a colleague as an on-off matter—either you are somebody's colleague or not—and we think that one has to be a colleague in the most maximal sense possible, then perhaps it would be best to conclude that a robot cannot be anybody's colleague.

However, if we think that there are different ways of being colleagues and that the idea of being somebody's colleague admits of degrees, this conclusion seems less outrageous. When the philosopher Helen Ryland (2021) discusses whether robots can be our friends, she suggests that there are different kinds of friendships and that friendship admits of different degrees: we can be somebody's friend to a lesser or greater degree. Robots might not be able to be our friends to a maximal degree, Ryland suggests. But they can be our friends to a certain degree. We could follow Ryland's lead and say that while robots can perhaps not fulfill all the conditions for being a colleague to a maximal degree, they can fulfill some of the conditions—at least conditions 1 and 2 in the Betzler and Löschke theory—to some degree.

It might even be claimed that robots could fulfill condition 3 to some degree. When the soldiers in the military bomb disposal unit treated Boomer to a military funeral and wanted to give Boomer two Medals of Honor, they seemed to treat Boomer as if this robot had a similar status as some of the humans in the team. So, from their point of view, perhaps they would be inclined to say that Boomer fulfilled the third condition too.

This last idea might be met with skepticism. Nevertheless, whether or not robots could fulfill condition 3, let us draw the following tentative conclusion: robots could at least fulfill conditions 1 and 2, doing so perhaps not to the same degree as humans could, but at least to a sufficient degree that they could qualify as being colleagues. With this tentative first conclusion in place, let us now turn to the question of whether a robot could also be a *good* colleague.

## Can a Robot Be a Good Colleague?

As noted earlier, when philosophers discuss whether robots could be our friends or perhaps even our romantic partners, one type of question they sometimes discuss is whether robots can behave in the ways that friends and romantic partners are supposed to behave. In other words, philosophers—as well as other researchers interested in human-robot interaction—have reflected on what might be called performative criteria for qualifying as a good friend or romantic partner (De Graaf, 2016; Danaher, 2019b). Some have argued that robots could—or in the future will be able to—behave in at least some of the key ways that friends are supposed to behave. Perhaps robots could even be made to behave in some of the ways a romantic partner is supposed to behave. If this is correct, then at least at a behavioral level, we could conclude that robots could potentially be good friends for us human beings. As noted earlier, this would be a little bit like a Turing test. The thing tested would not be whether machines can think (which is what Turing was interested in). Rather, the test here is whether robots can imitate what we associate with good friends or romantic partners.

John Danaher (2019b), who was mentioned previously, argues that it is plausible to suppose that robots could be made to treat us in the ways that good friends treat their friends. According to Danaher, if we follow this "ethical behaviorist" approach, we should conclude that a robot could be a good friend or perhaps even a romantic partner for a human being. Notably, lots of people who have been using the "Replika" chatbot seem to agree. Many of them have felt that this chatbot had become a good friend to them because of how the chatbot behaves in its interactions with them (Nyholm, 2023, chapter 9).

In a paper Jilles Smids and I wrote, we reflected on what kinds of behavior people value in good colleagues (Nyholm & Smids, 2020). We argued that when it comes to whether somebody is a good colleague, among the things we tend to care about is precisely how people behave in the workplace and how they perform in their role as our co-workers. From this point of view, we argued, it is not altogether implausible that a robot could be a good colleague—at least by the kinds of behavioral criteria we were considering.

What kind of behavioral criteria matters when it comes to whether somebody is a good colleague? And how can one decide what criteria matter? When Smids and I approached these questions, we first brainstormed about what one associates with being a good colleague. We then ran the points we came up with by various colleagues—first some colleagues of ours who are organizational psychologists and then various colleagues at a large philosophy conference, where we presented our paper. On the basis of this brainstorming and the feedback from our colleagues, Smids and I came up with—among other things—the following set of behavioral criteria for how a good colleague should behave or perform in the workplace. Being good colleagues should ideally involve, among other things:

(a) Working well together to achieve desired outcomes and goals specifically related to the work in question
(b) Being able to engage in pleasant, informal conversations, to help to keep work pleasant

(c) Not harassing or bullying colleagues, but instead treating each other respectfully
(d) Providing mutual help and support as needed
(e) Learning and developing together
(f) "Consistency," meaning that the colleagues are not constantly replaced with new colleagues but that they work together over extended periods of time
(g) Being reliable and trustworthy
(h) Being sensitive to how one's colleagues seem to be doing and adjusting one's work-related interaction accordingly
(i) Sharing work-related values and being motivated to honor these values in the joint work (Nyholm & Smids, 2020, p. 2177)

These criteria on what it is to be a good colleague can be interpreted as specifying how good colleagues should behave in workplace settings. The question now is whether robots could behave in these ways—or at least in some of these ways. Here, too, we might follow Helen Ryland's lead and think of this as something that could be a matter of degree—rather than an all-or-nothing matter.

We might think, for example, that humans and robots could work well together in ways that help to achieve the goals related to the work in question (criterion (a)). With impressive recent developments in what chatbots and language models can do—as illustrated by the examples of Google's LaMDA language model and the Replika chatbot (Nyholm, 2023)—it is plausible that robots could behave in ways that make it seem as if they engage in pleasant conversation with the humans in the workplace (criterion (b)). Robots could behave in ways that avoid any kinds of harassment or bullying of their human colleagues (criterion (c)). The humans and the robots could behave in ways that mutually help and support each other (criterion (d)). The humans and robots could learn and develop together over time in the workplace (criterion (e)). The humans and the robots could work together over long periods of time, so that there is consistency in the workplace (criterion (f)). The robots could be reliable and—at least in a minimal sense—trustworthy (criterion (g)). The robots could be designed to be to some degree sensitive to how the human beings appear to be doing (criterion (h)). And the robots could be designed to behave in ways that are aligned with the values associated with the given kinds of work (criterion (i)).

Perhaps workplace robots will not be able to fully live up to these criteria for being a good colleague in the way that a fellow human colleague is able to do. They might only partly be able to live up to some of these criteria. But then again, they might be able to outperform humans along some of these dimensions—at least in certain kinds of situations.

If we understand the criteria outlined earlier in a behavioral way—that is, if we see them as related to how good colleagues should perform in the workplace—then it is not altogether implausible to suppose that robots could live up to these criteria, at least to some extent. So, if whether somebody is a good colleague is a matter of degree—and an ideal that can be realized in different ways, perhaps depending on what kind of work is at issue—then the idea that robots can be good colleagues is not altogether crazy. They might work well together with the humans in the workplace, be able to behave in ways that make work pleasant, be reliable and so on.

Accordingly, not only does it make a certain amount of sense to say that a robot could be a colleague (at least to a certain degree) according to the conditions for being a colleague discussed in the previous section, but it also makes a certain amount of sense to think that a robot could be a *good* colleague (at least to a certain degree) according to the criteria for how a good colleague should behave in the workplace discussed in this section.

But what if we not only think about how good colleagues should behave in workplaces, but we also consider collegial values that are not only about how one behaves or performs in the workplace? Is it then still plausible to think that robots could have relationships with human beings in workplaces that help to realize the values that we associate with good collegial relationships?

## Can Collegial Values Like Solidarity and Recognition Be Realized Within Human-Robot Workplace Interactions?

To reflect further on whether robots can be part of workplace relationships that realize important work-related values, let us now return to Monika Betzler and Jürg Löschke's (2021) more general discussion of what it is to be a colleague and what values can be realized within good collegial relationships. It is important to note here that what Betzler and Löschke are interested in are interpersonal values associated with work relationships in particular, as opposed to more general interpersonal values. The values that they focus on as particularly important to realize within good collegial relationships—where being colleagues is understood in the way discussed earlier—are the following two: collegial solidarity and collegial recognition.

To illustrate these ideas, it is useful to return to how Betzler and Löschke understand what it is for two (or more) individuals to be colleagues. Two out of three conditions should hold: the individuals have the same or relevantly similar (1) type of work content or domain of activity, (2) institutional affiliation or common purpose and/or (3) status or level of responsibility. For example, two university professors might have the same type of work, be part of the same institution and have the same status and level of responsibility. Or two bakers might both bake for the same bakery and have the same status and responsibilities. Or two fellow musicians might be playing in the same orchestra with the same responsibilities. And so on.

When people relate to each other in such ways, they are in a unique position to give each other solidarity and due recognition—given their understanding of the kind of work their colleagues are doing, their shared experiences with the given kind of work, their ability to judge how well the colleague performs and what it takes to reach that level, and so on. Other people who do not relate to them in these ways will be less able to offer the kind of collegial solidarity and due recognition than colleagues who relate to each other in the ways Betzler and Löschke describe do. The question now is whether robots could show collegial solidarity and give due recognition to human beings they work alongside in the workplace. My suggestion is that we should be skeptical about this.

Now, if we understand showing solidarity and recognition in a purely behavioral way, then perhaps robots could be made to behave as if they offer solidarity and recognition to the humans in the work team. They could perhaps pass a form of Turing test for whether they are able to convincingly imitate or behave as if they can show solidarity and give recognition. Moreover, when it comes to recognition of good work, a robot might be able to track quantifiable achievements on the part of a human in the team in a way that might even outperform the other humans' ability to keep track of whatever performance indicators might be concerned. A robot in a warehouse, for example, might be better able than a human to count how many boxes a human worker has packed, how long it has taken and so on. But solidarity and recognition are not only about behavior (or the imitation of human actions) or the quantification of easy-to-measure performance indicators.

In addition, the humans in the work team might feel some sort of solidarity toward the robots in the team, and they might give what they think is due recognition to the robots. Recall the soldiers in the military unit that Boomer the bomb disposal robot was part of. These soldiers showed what seemed like a form of solidarity when Boomer was damaged, and there was a question of whether to retire that robot and replace it with another robot. They gave Boomer what might seem like a mark of recognition when they wanted to give Boomer a military funeral and two Medals of Honor when the robot was permanently destroyed. But what if these soldiers would want Boomer to give them solidarity and due recognition?

Showing solidarity and giving due recognition, as I understand these ideas, require that one has an ability to understand another person's situation. It also requires that one has certain emotional capacities. Solidarity and recognition are not merely two forms of behavior. Nor are they two forms of mindless information processing. For example, if one professor, baker, musician, soldier, logistics warehouse worker and so on has solidarity with another professor, baker and so on, then this involves their having an understanding—and the appropriate forms of emotions and internal attitudes—in relation to their colleague. Likewise, to give a fellow professor, baker and so on due recognition, we need to understand and have a sense of what is involved in being a professor, baker and so on worthy of recognition.

A robot—or any other form of AI system currently in existence—lacks the capacity for understanding. And it lacks any capacities for emotions or other forms of inner attitudes. They can perhaps imitate some behavioral patterns associated with understanding and emotions. But they merely process and respond to information—they register inputs with their sensors and respond with outputs (Nyholm, 2020). This is not the same as having an understanding of another person. And it is not the same as responding with the appropriate emotions and other attitudes. Therefore, I take it that robots cannot give human co-workers the kind of solidarity and recognition that might be due to a colleague.

Regarding the idea of seeking recognition from a robot or other AI system, this is a topic that the philosopher of technology and emotions researcher Catrin Misselhorn (2021) discusses in a recent book of hers. She argues that if we seek recognition from a robot or any other currently existing AI technology, we are in effect treating ourselves as if we were mere things.

Why does Misselhorn think this? She thinks that we then treat ourselves as if we do not have minds—as if we don't have thoughts, feelings, attitudes and so on—that we wish to communicate to others who have minds with whose help they can understand and empathize with what is on our minds. If we seek recognition from a robot, according to Misselhorn, we act as if our own minds (our thoughts, feelings, attitudes and so on) do not matter and as if we might as well be interacting with things that could not possibly understand us but that could simply register and process information about us in the way that modern technologies are able to do. As Misselhorn sees things, we do a form of harm to ourselves if we seek recognition from a robot. We fail to acknowledge and take seriously our human need for recognition from fellow human beings.

Is Misselhorn right that we treat ourselves as if we were a mere thing if we seek recognition from a robot? Are we in effect humiliating ourselves? As I see things, we can set those further questions aside when we reflect on whether the values of collegial solidarity and recognition can be realized within workplace interaction with robots. It is enough to ask whether we could get what we want and value when we want and value solidarity and recognition in interaction with robots. And since these two things—solidarity and recognition—clearly seem to require that the other has a capacity for understanding and certain forms of emotions and attitudes, this is enough for it to not be possible to realize these values within interaction with robots. It is not possible since robots lack understanding and the right forms of emotional capacities and attitudes.

Perhaps in the future there will be robots or other AI systems that are truly intelligent, that have understanding, and that have the kinds of emotional capacities and sentience that human beings have. Perhaps. But currently most experts from different fields agree that the robots and AI systems we have today are not in possession of such capacities. In order to create technologies that would be able to truly understand things or have humanlike emotions or attitudes, very significant technological developments would be necessary. So other than in science fiction, we should not expect to realize human interpersonal values in our interaction with robots if those interpersonal values require that the involved parties have minds, understanding, emotional capacities and so on. This applies to interpersonal values both within and outside of the workplace.

## Concluding Discussion

The three theses I have argued for point in slightly different directions. On the one hand, I have argued that robots could be our colleagues by at least two out of the three criteria presented by Betzler and Löschke and that on a behavioral level, robots could even be good colleagues. At least, they can be made to behave in many of the ways we expect good colleagues to behave in. On the other hand, I have just argued that some key values we associate with collegial relationships—namely solidarity and recognition—cannot be realized with interaction between humans and robots in workplaces. Those who are suspicious and critical of any ideas about human-robot interaction that sound like they could be part of science fiction would surely be quick to endorse the third thesis I have argued for. But they may think that the first two theses are problematic. I will end by considering possible push-back against those two earlier theses.

Regarding the idea that robots could be colleagues in any sense, one possible objection to that thesis is that (1) this would imply that robots work in the ways that human beings do, whereas (2) robots do not actually work in the ways that human beings do. Recall that I suggested that we understand work, roughly, as being the performance of certain tasks in exchange for monetary (or other) rewards, in accordance with a contract or other agreement. It might be suggested that robots do not get paid for their work and are not "hired" to do the work they do based on a contract. Since they do not work in the way that we do, it might be argued, it cannot be that robots can be our colleagues at work.

I think this is a serious objection to the idea that robots could be our colleagues. But I also think there are things that could be said in response to this objection. The first thing is that, in theory, robots can become legal persons—if laws are changed so as to make it possible for robots to be legal persons. They could then become able to earn income, and they could also become able to enter into contracts. So even though robots are not legal persons by current legal arrangements, things could be changed in our legal systems so that robots could work in the sense of work that I defined already.

A second possible response to this objection is that Betzler and Löschke's three conditions for being a colleague could be interpreted in a way that leaves it open whether all individuals who are said to be colleagues by those standards need to be able to work according to the definition of work I am operating within this chapter. That is, while perhaps only the humans involved work by this definition, the robots involved might still have the same tasks, be part of the same organization, and perhaps even have the same status or responsibilities in some sense (though the last condition does not have to be fulfilled since only two out of three conditions need to be fulfilled in order to count as a colleague).

The idea that robots might be our work colleagues without actually working in the sense of earning an income and having a contract might bring to mind the idea of robots as slaves that was mentioned in the introduction when I briefly quoted Aristotle at the beginning of the chapter. Actually, one very influential voice in the ethics of AI—the AI ethicist Joanna Bryson—has a famous paper that is even called "Robots Should Be Slaves" (Bryson, 2010). I can imagine that readers familiar with that paper would here be reminded of it. So let's end by briefly saying something about that paper in this context.

Bryson argues that it is unethical to treat robots in anthropomorphizing ways—that is, in ways that attribute human attributes to the robots. Robots, Bryson (2010) argues, are property we own and tools we create for our own ends. That is how we should regard and treat robots. That is, we should regard them as our property and tools that work for us—in the way that some people of the past have regarded and treated the people who were their slaves. Bryson thinks that it is horrible that any human beings were ever slaves. But a robot is not a human being. And so there is nothing wrong with treating—rather, it is perfectly correct to treat—a robot as a mere piece of property or a mere tool. From this point of view, it might seem that it could be considered unethical to regard any robot as a colleague or to even regard it as a good colleague.

It should be noted here that Bryson thinks that if we could create robots that had true intelligence or that could think or feel, then it would be unethical to treat those robots as slaves. We might then have duties toward these robots, and perhaps they even become our equals. However, we should avoid creating any such robots, Bryson argues. Anybody who shares this point of view would be inclined, I am assuming, to feel uncomfortable with the idea that robots could be our colleagues or that they could ever be considered as good colleagues.

In response to this, I will end by saying three things. Firstly, I have some sympathy with the idea that Bryson defends that it is best to avoid creating any robots or other AI technologies toward which (or whom?) we would have any direct obligations like we have obligations to humans and other living beings. Secondly, however, it might still be true—and I think it is still true—that robots can live up to the conditions formulated by Betzler and Löschke for when some individual counts as a colleague. And it might then still be that robots can live up to some of the behavioral criteria for how a good colleague should behave. In other words, perhaps we should not have robots as colleagues. But that does not necessarily mean that we cannot have robots as colleagues or that robots cannot be good colleagues, at least on a behavioral level. Thirdly, there are already—as noted earlier—people who regard robots they work alongside as their colleagues and indeed as good colleagues, worthy of various kinds of honors or recognition. So even if Bryson were right that there is something regrettable when people anthropomorphize robots, we have to think about how we should deal with the fact that people have those kinds of responses to robots. Moreover, anthropomorphizing interactions with robots will probably happen more and more as robots and AI people are getting more and more advanced in their capabilities and start being used in more and more workplaces.

In general, I think that we need to recognize that when robots or other AI technologies start to acquire capabilities that lead human beings to respond to these robots in social ways—regarding the robots as their friends, colleagues and so on—we are faced with a difficult and slightly awkward situation from an ethical point of view (Nyholm, 2020, 2023). The more humanlike technologies become, the more ethically ambiguous it becomes how it is ethically correct to interact with these technologies. The more something looks and acts like a mere tool and the less it inspires any social response in human beings, the less ethically problematic it is to treat the technology as a mere tool toward which we have no reason to interact in a social sort of way.

Robots that trigger social responses in human beings are an ethical challenge we have to deal with as we move into an even more highly technological future. It increasingly becomes important to rethink what is possible in terms of what kinds of relationships humans and robots or other technologies might have with each other. Robots in workplaces constitute one key instance of a case where old categories—for example, those of being a colleague or even a good colleague—might need to be used in new ways or where perhaps new concepts and categories are needed.

## References

Aristotle. (1957). *Politica* (D. Ross, Ed.). Oxford University Press.

Betzler, M., & Löschke, J. (2021). Collegial relationships. *Ethical Theory and Moral Practice*, *24*(1), 213–229.

Bryson, J. J. (2010). Robots should be slaves. In Y. Wilks (Ed.), *Close engagements with artificial companions* (pp. 63–74). John Benjamins.

Carpenter, J. (2015). *Culture and human-robot interactions in militarized spaces*. Routledge.

Danaher, J. (2019a). *Automation and utopia*. Harvard University Press.

Danaher, J. (2019b). The philosophical case for robot friendship. *Journal of Posthuman Studies*, *3*(1), 5–24.

De Graaf, M. (2016). An ethical evaluation of human-robot relationships. *International Journal of Social Robotics*, *8*(4), 589–598.

Devecka, M. (2013). Did the Greeks believe in their robots? *The Cambridge Classical Journal*, *59*, 52–69.

Garber, M. (2013). Funerals for Fallen Robots. *The Atlantic*, https://www.theatlantic.com/technology/archive/2013/09/funerals-for-fallen-robots/279861/

Gordon, J.-S., & Nyholm, S. (2021). Ethics of artificial intelligence. *Internet Encyclopedia of Philosophy*. https://iep.utm.edu/ethic-ai/

Groom, V., & Nass, C. (2007). Can robots be teammates? Benchmarks in human—robot teams. *Interaction Studies*, *8*(3), 483–500.

Ljungblad, S., Kotrbova, J., Jacobsson, M., Cramer, H., & Niechwiadowicz, K. (2012). Hospital robot at work: Something alien or an intelligent colleague? In *Proceedings of the ACM 2012 conference on computer supported cooperative work* (pp. 177–186). ACM.

Misselhorn, C. (2021). *Künstliche Intelligenz und Empathie*. Reclam.

Nyholm, S. (2020). *Humans and robots: Ethics, agency, and anthropomorphism*. Rowman & Littlefield International.

Nyholm, S. (2023). *This is technology ethics: An introduction*. Wiley-Blackwell.

Nyholm, S., & Smids, J. (2020). Can a robot be a good colleague? *Science and Engineering Ethics*, *26*(4), 2169–2188.

Royakkers, L., & van Est, R. (2015). *Just ordinary robots: Automation from love to war*. CRC Press.

Russell, S., & Norvig, P. (2010). *Artificial intelligence: A modern approach*. Prentice Hall.

Ryland, H. (2021). It's friendship, Jim, but not as we know it: A degrees-of-friendship view of human-robot friendships. *Minds and Machines*, *31*(3), 377–393.

Sauppé, A., & Mutlu, B. (2015). The social impact of a robot co-worker in industrial settings. In *Proceedings of the 33rd annual ACM conference on human factors in computing systems* (pp. 3613–3622). ACM.

Smids, J., Nyholm, S., & Berkers, H. (2021). Robots in the workplace: A threat to—or opportunity for—meaningful work? *Philosophy and Technology*, *33*(3), 503–522.

# 2 Creative Machine-Human Collaboration

## Toward a Cybernetic Approach to Artificial Intelligence and Machine Learning Techniques in the Creative Arts

*Stephen Roddy*

### Recent Developments in AI Applied to Art

There have been giant leaps forward in the application of cutting-edge artificial intelligence (AI) and machine learning (ML) and more specifically deep learning (DL), technologies in creative and cultural industries in recent years. These changes have been felt in the visual arts and music in particular. After a brief technical overview later, the impact of these technologies on the contemporary landscape in both fields is explored with reference to their historical antecedents.

Audry's succinct description describes ML algorithms as processes that underpin "computational systems that are biologically inspired, statistically driven, agent-based networked entities that program themselves" (Audry, 2021). Within this somewhat broad definition, we find a myriad of ML model architectures that can be adapted to a wide range of tasks in the creative arts. Large language models with transformer-based architectures like T5 (Raffel et al., 2020) and the GPT series (Heikkilä, 2023; Brown et al., 2020), have revolutionized the production of human-like text and AI-driven chatbots, ChatGPT and Bard in particular, are whipping up a flurry of fevered speculation about the nature of machine intelligence (Warzel, 2023). Generative models for visual production like Midjourney (Midjourney, 2023), DALL-E 2 (OpenAI, 2021a), Imagen (Google, 2022a) and Parti (Google, 2022b) generate a wide range of imagery from simple text prompts. DALL-E 2 and Imagen employ diffusion models, which operate by destroying their training data through the addition of Gaussian noise before learning to recover the original data through a process of reversal (Dhariwal & Nichol, 2021). Stable Diffusion v1 (Rombach et al., 2022) also shows promising results for image generation and modification. Image modification converts simplistic sketches into detailed artworks, something that Nvidia's GauGAN2 can achieve in close to real time (Park et al., 2019). Both GauGAN2 and Parti employ the Generative Adversarial Network (GAN) architecture introduced by Goodfellow et al. (2014). Other comparable models

DOI: 10.4324/9781003299875-2

include StyleGAN3 (Karras et al., 2021) and VQGAN (Esser et al., 2021), a variant of which is used in Parti. These models can be combined with CLIP (OpenAI, 2021b) to handle text prompts for image generation tasks.

There have been developments in the production of sound and music too. MuseNet adopts a similar approach to GPT-2 and is trained on and designed to produce MIDI files that can be synthesized or mapped to a sonic output later (Payne, 2021). The Magenta project has developed Variational Autoencoders or VAE (Roberts et al., 2018) for generating music that is designed to work with MIDI data. They have also developed a technique branded differentiable digital signal processing or DDSP for transforming the sounds of musical instruments (Engel et al., 2020). This approach works on raw audio waveforms, as opposed to MIDI files, in a similar fashion to OpenAI's WaveNet (Oord et al., 2016), which was a breakthrough model for raw audio generation in 2016. A similar approach is employed by OpenAI's Jukebox (Dhariwal et al., 2020), which uses a VAE architecture trained on raw audio files to generate music across a wide variety of genres. There is now an ever-expanding range of websites and applications that use ML technologies to creative ends.

Artists have been working with AI since at least the late 1960s when Harold Cohen began work on AARon, a rule-based system from image generation that simulated cognitive primitives thought by Cohen to underpin drawing and painting (Cohen, 1982). Lejaren Hiller and Leonard Issacson's Illliac Suite, a 1957 string quartet in four movements, is thought to be the first computer-assisted composition (Hiller & Isaacson, 1957). The pair devised increasingly complex compositional methods for each movement beginning with some simple harmonic rules for the first movement and ending with the application of Markov Chains for the fourth. In a similar fashion to Cohen, David Cope began work on his experiments in musical intelligence (EMI) system in 1981 (Cope, 1992), which generated music by analyzing musical input data for core signifiers of the works that could be retained during the recombination of musical sequences to create novel works.

The recent ML boom, driven by the rise in availability of computing hardware like high-performing GPUs and cloud computing infrastructures, the availability of rich big datasets, and the improved effectiveness of DL techniques, has led to a flood of new artists working with AI and ML systems. The techniques adopted during this boom period stand in stark contrast to earlier artists like Harold Cohen and David Cope who worked with rule-based AI, sometimes referred to as Good Old Fashioned AI or GOFAI or artists working in a visual medium like Frieder Nake and Herbert Franke who were interested in computational systems more generally.

Ahmed Elgammal (2019) argues that the work being produced in this epoch is a form of conceptual art because the focus is on the creative process rather than the piece produced and the collaboration between artist and machine required to produce it. Miller (2019) describes how Alexander Mordvintsev's Deep Dream marked a turning point for AI art. This system creates dream-like imagery by applying a convolutional neural network to amplify and iterate upon patterns in input images. Important works in this epoch include Mike Tyka's (2018) Portraits of Imaginary People, which used a GAN trained on photos of faces collected from Flickr.com to generate new faces of people who do not exist. Mario Klingemann's (2017) Imposture Series meanwhile produced works with a GAN trained on varied combinations of stick figures and imagery harvested from the internet. Refik Anadol's (2016) Machine Hallucination series uses huge sets of visual data (e.g., photos from the International Space Station or photos of natural phenomena and landscapes) to train GAN-type models and then renders his pieces as walks through the model's latent space: the compressed representation of the features from the original data that has been learned by the model. Memo Akten's (2017) Hello World trains a VAE on a live video feed allowing the user to change model hyperparameters in real time as it trains. Pindar Van Arman's Cloud Painter project uses DL techniques to teach robots to paint like people (Miller, 2019). These changes have impacted markets in the creative and cultural industries. In 2018, the arts collective Obvious sold a visual artwork created with a GAN they sourced on GitHub. It sold for $432,000 at Christie's, which was particularly problematic given that the GAN in question was written by AI artist Robbie Barat, a teenager at the time, who was excluded from the profits of the sale (Miller, 2019; Flynn, 2018).

A notable early application of neural networks in the creative arts is Rebecca Feibrink's Wekinator (Fiebrink et al., 2009), which uses neural networks to learn bespoke mapping strategies from real-time control data inputs to the parameters of a given multimedia system like a synthesizer. In 2017 Taryn Southern and Benoît Carré's SKYGGE project both produced albums that incorporated ML techniques. Southern's I AM AI made use of IBM's Watson Beat and tools provided by amper.com (Jancer, 2018), while SKYGGE's Hello World worked with tools created by flow machines to produce his pieces (SKYGGE, 2017). That same year Dadabots began releasing works that involved WaveNet-style raw audio models trained on a variety of music but particularly Black Metal (Zukowski & Carr, 2018). In 2018 Ash Koosha explored AI on Return 0 (Cardew, 2018), and in 2019 Auxuman (Fry, 2021), an AI collective co-founded by Koosha, began monthly musical releases. Lee Gamble (Quarshie, 2021), Mouse on Mars (Sherburne, 2021) and Arca (Darville, 2020) have incorporated a variety of ML techniques into their music and Hexorcismos' Transfiguración devised a novel approach to synthesizing audio with GANs (Kirn, 2020). Bob Sturm and Oded Ben-Tal are working with real-world traditional music practitioners to produce novel new musical scores using ML/DL techniques (Miller, 2019). Another highly original approach is Holly Herndon's Holly+, an AI-driven vocal deepfake tool that allows users to make music their own music using her voice (Holly, 2021).

While the works of musical artists engaging with ML technologies can be contextualized within a larger tradition of computer music and computational art more broadly (Miller, 2019), neural networks and ML techniques only entered the picture in a music composition context in the late 1980s with the publication of pioneering work by Lewis (1988) and Todd (1988). Following this, David Tudor's (1995) Neural Synthesis N° 6–9, was a collection of pieces composed with a hardware synthesizer designed for Tudor by Forrest Warthman, Mark Holler and Mark Thorson. The synthesizer was built around an analog neural network microchip: the Intel 80170NX neural processor or electronically trainable analog neural network (ETANN) (Kuivila, 2004). Eck and Schmidhuber (2002) would be the first to apply long short-term memory models (LSTMs) in a musical context and with the DL boom of the early 2010s a wide range of ML applications in both music and the digital arts emerged. While the application of ML to the arts is a more recent development, its focus and development have nonetheless been shaped and constrained by historical forces, which have defined how we conceptualize, design and interact with intelligent machines.

## Problematic Foundations

The human relationship to machines and the concept of intelligent machines, in particular, has long been shaped by a central anxiety about the eventual replacement of humans by machines. In *Machines Who Think: A Personal Inquiry Into the History and Prospects of Artificial Intelligence*, Pamela McCorduck lays out a scathing criticism of, among other things, the master-servant dynamic that underpins a lot of our thinking about intelligent machines (McCorduck, 1979). She highlights how even the word "robot" is coded with these values having first appeared to describe the factory-fabricated android servants in Karel Čapek's play, *R.U.R.* (Rossumovi Univerzální Roboti—Rossum's Universal Robots). The term was dreamed up by Čapek's brother Josef and is derived from the Czech word for "servitude." It is also worth noting that the titular robots of the play revolt against their human masters, bringing about the extinction of humanity. The anxiety that one day intelligent machines we have created and indentured will rise up and turn the tables on their human masters has been a theme in the cultural and literary depictions of the robot since its very inception. Even earlier in 1872 Samuel Butler's *Erewhon* (see Butler, 2015), specifically the three chapters that constitute *The Book of the Machine*, introduced the idea that machines might become conscious through a Darwinian process of natural selection and thus learn to self-replicate also. While he would later come to believe that a mechanistic model of the organism would render it incapable of consciousness (Breuer, 1975), his writings in *The Book of the Machine* suggested that intelligent machines were to be feared as a dangerous threat, destined to gradually supersede and replace humanity as a dominant force.

The AI takeover would become a recurring theme in 20th-century science fiction as writers and creators who, following Butler, explored and expanded upon the idea across a wide range of media. While Isaac Asimov famously rejected this notion, the theme appears in highly influential works by Stanisław Lem (Lem, 2021), Philip K. Dick (Dick, 1968) and Harlan Ellison (Ellison, 1967) that would in turn influence landmark works by filmmakers like Stanley Kubrick, Ridley Scott and James Cameron (Roberts, 2016).

The concept of the "technological singularity" was introduced by John von Neumann (Shanahan, 2015) and expanded by Alvin Toffler (Toffler, 1970). It developed into a cohesive vision in the writings of Vernor Vinge (Vinge, 1993) and Ray Kurzweil (Kurzweil, 2005) and would eventually be given a cursory mathematical formalization by Nick Bostrom (2014). The idea generally goes that our continually improving computing technologies will soon lead to the emergence of runaway superintelligences that radically reshape society and humanity. The idea is not without its critics. Pein (2018) provides criticism of both Vinge and Kurzweil, pointing out the lack of a sound scientific basis for their predictions about the singularity and attacking the cult-like nature of the movement that has grown up around those predictions. Benthall (2017) uses a Bayesian model to demonstrate that the probability of Bostrom's intelligence explosion actually happening, based as it is on the advancement of recursively self-improving AI algorithms, is negligible given the importance of hardware and data to the growth of intelligence. Kurzweil's singularity is one wherein, rather than replacing humans, superintelligent AI will enhance and improve humanity as it integrates more closely with it. It eventually leads to humans uploading scanned copies of their brains (and therefore minds according to Kurzweil) into these superintelligent machines thus achieving a form of techno-mediated immortality. By contrast, for Vinge, superintelligent machines are a dangerous threat and, in the best-case scenario, the one in which they don't simply wipe out all human life, they must be bound as "godlike slaves" to the will of their human masters. This is echoed by Bostrom who sees it as imperative that we solve the "control problem" to prevent an existential catastrophe. His various methods for controlling intelligent machines include containment, stunting, self-destruct scenarios and a kind of machine eugenics that might select for domesticity and normative alignment. Vinge and Bostrom's singularity scenarios are underpinned by a sense of anxiety that humans will be replaced by machines and as such humanity must double down in its role as subjugator, ruthlessly enforcing the master-servant dynamic that already defines so much of the relationship of humans to machines.

As McCorduck points out, this dynamic has been with human thought for a long time. We see early descriptions of automata, mechanical humans, in the 4th-century BCE Daoist text the *Liezi* attributed to the 5th-century philosopher Lie Yukou (Richey, 2011). The artificer Yan Shi creates a wooden automaton that can dance and sing. The automaton attracts the ire of King Mu when it breaks from the established protocols of the court and begins to wink and advance toward the ladies of the court causing Yan Shi to take him apart. Both a master-servant dynamic and a level of anxiety with regard to the robot breaking from its assigned role in this hierarchy are on display here. It is also noteworthy that this early depiction of an automaton presents it as a creative being: a skilled singer and dancer. This is of course because it was created to entertain the powerful, in this case, King Mu, to win favor or reward for his creator. In the Iliad, we again see the master-servant dynamic at play when Homer describes Hephaestus' servants as intelligent and articulate young women, wrought from gold and portrayed as supportive of their master's every move (Lattimore, 1894). Reflecting on depictions of automata in the Iliad, Aristotle speculated in his *Politics* that they might lead to the abolition of slavery by essentially taking over all labor (Aristotle & Ellis, 1888). Another of Hephaestus' creations, the Greek god Talos, is, in a popular telling of the story, forged to protect the goddess Europa who resides on the island of Crete, from pirates and aggressors. Created for one specific purpose, he diligently carries it out never breaking from protocol or upturning the rules (Mayor, 2018).

In a similar fashion to the musical automaton created by Yan Shi in the *Liezi*, Hero of Alexandria (c. AD 62) produced illustrated designs for a range of automata, a good deal of which were musical (Woodcroft, 1851). His *Pneumatics*, building upon and interpreting a text of the same name by Philo of Byzantium (250 BC), provides detailed illustrated designs he produced for theatrical performances. It included an automaton that sounds a trumpet with compressed air, a singing blackbird and a trumpet playing Triton driven by a steam boiler, and two designs for altar organs, one blown by a windmill and another by annual labor (Woodcroft, 1851). His other surviving work *On Automata-Making* contains a range of designs for theatre automata. These were elaborate sets that could involve multiple moving figures, flowing liquids, mechanisms for producing sounds and often some type of fire. Both books were rediscovered during the renaissance and had great influence in the late Renaissance period (Steadman, 2021). Steadman highlights a sense of fun that surrounded automata in the Renaissance period, and this same sense of fun would reemerge from time to time in, for example, Vaucanson's Flute Player, Tambourine Player, and digesting duck automata in the 1700s and Joseph Faber's Fabulous Talking Machine or Euphonia exhibited in 1845 (Riskin, 2003). The earliest designs for truly programmable musical automata can be found in *The Book of Knowledge of Ingenious Mechanical Devices* by 13th-century polymath Ibn Ismail Ibn al-Razzaz Al-Jazari (Sharkey, 2007).

Many of these earlier automata were designed to entertain the rich and powerful with mechanistic analogies of music, dance and theatre. However, during the industrial revolution, the relationship between humans and machines would undergo another transformation. As Western nations began to transition from agriculture and artisan economies to heavy industries, the machines filling the factory floors of the West became critical components of economic infrastructure. Automated textile equipment, in particular, threatened the livelihoods of skilled weavers who could now be replaced with cheaper, less-skilled workers. In 19th-century England, this tension led to the rise of the Luddites, who protested the use of automation to circumvent fair labor practices. They are often remembered as technophobes who feared that they would be replaced by technological innovations. However, writing at the height of Reaganism and Thatcherism, David Linton parallels the economic, social and political conditions that gave rise to the Luddites with the contemporary trends of the day, arguing that their real issue was the increasingly excessive mistreatment and exploitation of labor by capital, of which the industrial machine became a symbol (Linton, 1985). The industrial revolution saw a trend toward wringing more labor from the individual worker at increasingly cheaper rates against a backdrop of continuous decline in both working conditions and living standards. In this landscape, the machine plays the role of diligent servant, the reliable capital of the industrialist class. These machines are not yet the intelligent agents discussed in ancient myth and modern science fiction, yet they have managed to capture and reproduce, in at least some coarse manner, skills and capacities that were previously thought to be uniquely human. This trend has continued into recent times where discussions about the drawbacks of AI in the workplace tend to focus on workers' fears of being replaced as a result of employers' deployment of technology to reduce labor costs and expand the bottom line.

Proponents of the Kurzwellian vision of AI utopia claim that as we approach the dawn of superintelligent AI, an increasing number of professions will be automated, effectively creating a post-labor world where machines do the work and humans reap the rewards, though these rewards tend to involve increased leisure time rather than any share of the profits generated (Skidelsky, 2020). While the old master-servant dynamic is at play here once again, it is also worth noting that superintelligent AIs described by Kurzweil, Vinge and Bostrom are by no means guaranteed to emerge. Alongside those discussed previously (Pein, 2018; Benthall, 2017), a wide range of thinkers, including Tozer (2020) and Colton (2020), argue that AI is radically different from human intelligence and is unlikely to ever operate in a similar or even comparable manner to human cognition.

## Promises and Limitations of AI

One early critic of human-level AI was Hubert Dreyfus. During the first wave of AI, Dreyfus argued that symbolically mediated cognitive processes require a context of tacit, informal background knowledge, in the sense indicated by Polanyi (1958), to render them meaningful (Dreyfus, 1965). A large portion of human knowledge, for example, domain-specific expertise, is tacit and informal and so cannot be represented symbolically. Thus, computation alone cannot account for knowledge with a tacit component (Dreyfus, 1976, 1992). The Chinese Room problem (Searle, 1980) showed that while rule-based computation may be sufficient to pass the Turing test, computation alone cannot account for how the symbols computed are assigned their meaning in a human mind. Harnad (1990) formalizes this as the symbol-grounding problem and argues that human experience is full of symbols—the meanings of which computation alone cannot account for. Ragnar Fjelland (2020) highlights that AI research since Dreyfus' original writings has shifted away from the GOFAI model of hard-coding systems of rules toward the design of neural network architectures that can learn relationships directly from a dataset. As such, we may be tempted to believe that these architectures can handle tacit knowledge, but they cannot. This is because the computer does not inhabit the same world as the human does. As such, for example, they do not deal with tacit knowledge as tacit knowledge but rather make arbitrary quantifications (i.e., encode a series of weights), which represent tacit knowledge as explicit knowledge or at least with an explicit formalization. For Fjelland, the DL revolution has not solved this problem because the problem is inherent to computation in general as opposed to AI/ML alone. The flip-side to this argument is that the degree to which we can ground an AI system in Fjelland's human world, mirrors the degree to which it can be said to have a human-like intelligence. But machine intelligence does not need to resemble human intelligence in to be effective as demonstrated in the capabilities of the systems discussed in this chapter. Nor should it need to in order for us to consider it a legitimate form of intelligence.

It may be more useful to think of machine intelligence as characterized less by the kinds of problem solving associated with human cognition and more with the kinds or problem solving we see in the expression of genetic code in the cells and tissues of the biological human substrate. Much of the value of ML/AI lies in the fact that it is different to human intelligence and can therefore do things that humans cannot, just as human intelligence can do things that machines cannot. The computer might not inhabit the human world, as Fjelland notes, but we humans increasingly inhabit the world of computing shaping our lives around it and carrying out much of our daily activities within a landscape of computation. As ML/AI technologies continue to restructure that digital landscape, so too will it restructure our lives and societies. In the end, for Fjelland, Dreyfus' critiques still hold in our current ML-driven epoch of AI. All this being said, the very idea of AI is predicated on the idea that certain machines have the capability to, at the very least, simulate some aspects of human cognition. This assumption of similarity between mind and machine, while present to some degree in the historical and mythological materials explored earlier, began to dominate culture in the 20th century.

## The Computer and the Mind

The period during and immediately after the Second World War saw huge advances in the field of computer science. A growing body of research seemed to be lending credence to the idea that the human mind was essentially an information processing machine. The Church-Turing thesis formalized the algorithm (Turing, 1936; Church, 1936) and Turing's theoretical universal machine (1936) claimed to simulate any algorithm with four simple rules. Shannon

(1938) argued that cognitive processes could be modeled by formalizing problem-solving across relay switch states with Boolean logic. McCulloch and Pitts (1943) devised logical models for neural networks and claimed mental activity thus could be modeled on a universal Turing machine. Von Neumann (1945) made it possible for a machine to program itself by storing programs in memory. Finally, at the first Hixon Symposium on Cerebral Mechanisms and Behaviour in 1948, thinkers like John Von Neumann, Warren McCulloch and Walter Pitts addressed talks to a multidisciplinary crowd of psychologists and computer scientists, in which they approached the brain, central nervous system and the mind in terms of computation (Gardner, 1987). This incitement, coupled with a growing sense of dissatisfaction with the methods and results of the prevailing behaviorist agenda in psychology, would contribute to the establishment of cognitive science as a distinct field of research. A key assumption on which the field was founded was the equivalence between mind and machine and the treatment of the human as an information processor. When AI emerged as a research field in the 1950s this model of cognition, what Putnam (1967) would later dub the classical computational theory of mind, was well established. Many of the key players in the early days of both cognitive science and computer science would also play roles in the development of the field. This line of thought prevailed in cognitive science until the 1980s when the impact of pioneering work in the field of cybernetics would be felt in cognitive science too. In fact, Hayles (1999) describes how cybernetics wrestled with this interpretation of the human, almost from its inception.

## Cybernetics and Cybernetic Art

Cybernetics originated with the work of mathematician Norbert Wiener who in his seminal 1948 text described it as the scientific study of control and communication in the animal and the machine (Wiener, 1948). He saw goal-directed, teleological behaviors such as self-regulation through feedback and feedforward loops as fundamental to electronic, mechanical and biological systems. Second-order cybernetics built on these ideas and driven by the work of Margaret Mead (1968) and Heinz Von Foerster (1984) introduced reflexive practices whereby the observing agent became a critical feature of the system. Maturana and Varela's autopoiesis (1980) and Stafford Beer's eventual reconfiguration of cybernetics from an operations research perspective as "the science of effective organization" (1972) would further expand the cybernetic horizon.

Cybernetic thought had a great influence on the arts, as demonstrated when in 1968 Jasia Reichardt curated an exhibition at the ICA in London titled Cybernetic Serendipity (Reichardt, 1968), which explored the relationship between technology and creativity. The exhibition was a watershed moment in new media arts. It brought together a wide range of artists, engineers, mathematicians and architects working within a cybernetic framework. It included contributions from, among others, Gordon Pask, Stafford Beer, Jeanne

Beaman, Frieder Nake, J. R. Pierce, Peter Zinovieff, Gustav Metzger, Nam June Paik, Frank Malina, Roger Dainton, John Cage, Karlheinz Stockhausen, Maughan S. Mason, A. R. Forrest and Margaret Masterman.

In the book accompanying the exhibition, Reichardt comments that "it may be difficult for an artist to imagine how he could possibly make use of a computer. The solution to the problem lies in collaboration" (Reichardt, 1968). This theme of collaboration between artist and machine is extended to the audience in Pask's *Colloquy of Mobiles* (Pask, 1969). Pask was a prominent cybernetic theorist with a deep interest in interactive installation art. His was an "aesthetically potent" environment that allowed its audience to actively engage in a discourse with a hierarchy of interacting mobiles. He favored a collaborative relationship between machine and human agents, a theme that was also present in his other works *Musicolour* and *SAKI* (Bird & DiPaolo, 2008).

Hayles (1999) points out that Cybernetics came together as a distinct field of research during the Macy conferences of 1946 to 1953 and in its initial wave was defined by a dialectic tension between the homeostasis, the ability of a system to maintain itself in a stable state through corrective feedback, and reflexivity, the tendency of a system to evolve, change and complexify in response to self-observation. Hayles highlights how the homeostasis camps were influenced by Claude Shannon's application of his information theory to cybernetics. They viewed the human as an information processing machine made noisy and erratic by the psychological complexity of subjective experience, and which may in time be replaced by a more efficient information processing machine. The reflexivity camp meanwhile felt that the subjectivity and psychological complexity of the human were to be embraced and accounted for in the negotiation of a more open and collaborative relationship between human and machine. Donald M. MacKay in particular viewed reflexivity as a reconciling agent between information and meaning, the latter of which is wholly unaccounted for in Shannon's information theory. The model of the human as an information processing machine, and an unreliable one at that, must inevitably lead to the conclusion that the human machine is fated for eventual replacement by a more efficient information processing machine. This theme reemerges again today in the cultural discourse around machine intelligence.

While Cybernetic Serendipity was generally well received, Usselmann (2003) reviews some of the dissenting voices at the time including some who rejected what they saw as a kind of techno-fetishist project to replace artists with machines and others who felt the event represented a kind of technocratic authoritarianism. Writing in 1971 Reichardt (Reichardt, 1971) criticized the tendency among journalists to ask if computers would replace humans, arguing that this emotionally charged line of questioning serves to obscure rather than illuminate the relationship between art and technology, further adding that the demystification of the art-making process does not demystify the result. For Reichardt a cybernetic approach to the arts is about human-machine collaboration as opposed to replacement of the artist or the use of machines by one class of humans to oppress another. To this degree, her view of the role of the human is closer to MacKay's than Shannon's and her collaborative take on cybernetics in the arts addresses both the master-servant dynamic and replacement anxiety.

While much of the work presented at Cybernetic Serendipity engaged with concepts and ideas from the field, the ten-track album released alongside the show, titled Cybernetic Serendipity Music, was also representative of the state of the art in experimental music as much as it represented human-machine collaboration. Alongside works by Zinovieff, Brün and Strang it included the fourth movement of Hiller and Isaacson's *Illiac Suite* (Hiller & Isaacson, 1957), an excerpt of Xenakis' *Stratégie* (1962) and an excerpt of Cage's *Cartridge Music* (Various Artists, 1968). Each of the pieces generally involved the use of a computer to generate musical materials through either the application of some ruleset or algorithm-like game theory on Xenakis' *Stratégie*, compositional processes hand-coded in FORTRAN on Herbert Brün's *Infraudibles*, or stochastic processes in Cage's *Cartridge Music*.

## Perspectives on Experimental Music

Boden (2004) argues that technologically mediated approaches in the creative arts necessarily involve the demystification of the creative process in explicit systems, models and rules. Furthermore, such approaches invariably involve the ceding of agency from artist to machine to some in regard. In the cases where the systems are overly constrained in terms of what outputs they can produce, creative works can become predictable and dull. This dialectic between what is boring and predictable and what is exciting touches all art but technologically mediated art especially (Nake, 2012). This becomes especially problematic in the current DL era, where, in a certain sense, predictability is fundamentally baked into the architecture of any algorithm. While ML models may generate new samples not present in their original input data, the set of all possible sample predictions is nonetheless defined and constrained by relationships and patterns in the original data, as encoded at training time by the architecture of the model. This throws up some interesting problems in the context of experimental music in particular. Cage (1961) held that, in the context of music composition, "an experimental action is one the outcome of which is not foreseen" and is "necessarily unique." It is not possible to take a body of known and well-understood musical data, and to create, by a process of prediction, an unforeseen musical output, which satisfies Cage's definition for experimental music. Furthermore, this problem cannot be solved by simply training a generative model on a corpus of experimental musical works. Important examples of musical works at the more experimental end of the spectrum tend to be highly specific one-of-a-kind pieces with unique reasons for existing and completely idiosyncratic aesthetics and internal organizational schemes. It is hard to argue that those patterns that are shared between Hugh Le Caine's *Dripsody* (1955) and Steve Reich's *It's Gonna Rain* (1965) are definitive of "experimental music" as an art form or similarly that any set of correlations between Xenakis' *Metastasis* (1955) and Halim El-Dabh's *Wire Recorder Piece* (1944) could be elaborated upon to generate a new experimental music composition. This is to say nothing of installed works, such as La Monte Young and Marian Zazeela's *Dream House* (1969) or Gordon Monahan's *Aeolian Silo* (1990), that cease to operate in the same manner when divorced from their context. These are all but unrepresentable in audio or video file formats and so it would prove exceptionally difficult to represent the original pieces in an ML dataset.

The patterns that exist across pieces of experimental music are much more loosely correlated than those that exist across more heavily regimented forms of musical expression like Western classical music and pop. The measure of distance between the familiar examples of experimental music is too large. Each one differs wildly from the next in terms of texture, timbre and form. Statistically speaking, a dataset comprising important or familiar experimental pieces would be inherently "noisy," in the sense described by Shannon's information theory, as there are few common patterns across pieces. Continuing with this metaphor, those patterns in the dataset that are stable and repetitive enough across examples to constitute a "signal" are fundamentally at odds with the spirit and intention of experimental music. Experimental music, in the sense described by Cage, cannot be produced as a prediction from a model trained on a musical dataset but could only result from a complex system or chaotic system in which the musical result cannot be foreseen. The idea of a musical result generated as a prediction from a model determined by other musical works is at odds with the Cagean understanding of experimental music, which favors randomness over predictability.

However, Cage's definition of experimental music, while historically privileged among Western Eurocentric scholars and artists, is not the only definition of experimental music. Critically, it is not a definition of, or approach to, experimental music that resonates within the current epoch of AI-driven art. Cage's musical ideas were influenced by his interest in Daisetz Suzuki's particular expression of Zen Buddhism, which was heavily influenced by William James' concept of "Pure Experience" as mapped to Zen in the early work of Nishida Kitarō (Roddy, 2017). George E. Lewis (1996) points out that Cage's approach, in its focus on unique and spontaneous chance operations in the present moment, eliminates personality, narrative, memory and history. In doing so it minimizes the works of prominent African American Jazz composers and improvisers like Charlie Parker, Dizzy Gillespie and Thelonious Monk who produced truly experimental music that embraced these elements in a live group improvisation context. He further highlights how Cage outright dismissed the value of Jazz in demarcating it from what he called "serious music" even when, as Born (1995) points out, Jazz musicians had incorporated core elements of experimental music practice since the 1950s. Lewis's take on experimental music is deeply indebted to Charlie Parker's idea of music as an expression of the lived experience of the players involved. Lewis sees collaborative musical improvisation steeped in personal narrative as an assertion of agency on behalf of the musicians involved. This is in stark contrast to Cage and followers whose master-servant model of composition called for the enforcement of control over the musical performer. This thinking underlies Lewis's development of Voyager, an interactive computer music environment that operates as a virtual improvising orchestra (Lewis, 2000) that was initially developed by combining principles from 1980s AI, and 1950s cybernetics, with sociomusical networks of free improvisation (Lewis, 2019, 2021). Debuted in 1987, Voyager would develop and evolve over the years, always operating as an autonomous computer-based system capable of improvising intelligently alongside human performers in a live context (Steinbeck, 2018). It is still an ongoing project and in 2022 Lewis began working with a team of researchers and practitioners at RNCM PRiSM to expand Voyager integrating AI/ML techniques (Royal Northern College of Music, 2022). For Lewis, collaborative improvisation is an assertion of agency that breaks from the master-servant dynamic, which pervades both human-machine collaboration and the relationship between composer and performer as reimagined by Cage and his followers. This contrasts with earlier musical machines like the automatons, which were designed to entertain rich and powerful masters, by reproducing set musical pieces to the rigid specification of the original designer/composer. Lewis's approach presents a model of experimental music that grants agency and autonomy to musical machines as improvisers of equal value alongside their flesh and blood collaborators.

## Current Trends and Future Directions

Lewis's approach to the use of intelligent machines as equal collaborators addresses both the issue of the master-servant dynamic and the fear that humans will be replaced by machines. It acknowledges and builds upon the reflexive approach of those second-order cyberneticists who believed human observers, with their complex histories, memories, personalities and individual autonomy constituted critical components of cybernetic systems. It takes this a step further however by extending the same courtesy to the machine and treating machine agents as equal collaborators that act with autonomy alongside their human counterparts. It further accounts for the cultural and social context in which these machine-human collaborators are performing, representing a highly novel and even compassionate approach to the use of intelligent machines in the creative arts. There are shades of Lewis's thinking emerging in the current epoch of AI/ML-driven art. Sougwen Chung's work explores equitable machine-human collaboration. Her piece *Omnia per Omnia* (Chung, 2018) approaches landscape painting as a collaboration between artist, robotic swarm and city. Špela Petrič's *PL'AI* (Petrič, 2020) allowed an AI-driven robot and a set of plants to interact with each other over a long timescale through play. The author's *Signal to Noise Loops* project foregrounds collaboration between city, machine and human in electronic music and audiovisual installation contexts (Roddy, 2023). The emergence of projects of this type that carry on the tradition of the cybernetics represented in George E. Lewis's work, free from the master-servant dynamic and anxiety of replacement, bode well for the future of collaboration between machines and humans in the creative arts.

## References


Akten, M. (2017). *Hello world* [interactive art]. https://www.memo.tv/works/learning-to-see/

Anadol, R. (2016). *Machine hallucinations* [visual art]. https://refikanadol.com/works/machine-hallucinations-nature-dreams/

Aristotle, & Ellis, W. (1888). *Politics: A treatise on government from the Greek of Aristotle*. Routledge.

Audry, S. (2021). *Art in the age of machine learning*. MIT Press.

Beer, S. (1972). *Brain of the firm*. Wiley.

Benthall, S. (2017). *Don't fear the reaper: Refuting Bostrom's superintelligence argument*. arXiv preprint arXiv:1702.08495. https://arxiv.org/abs/1702.08495

Bird, J., & Di Paolo, E. (2008). Gordon Pask and his maverick machines. *The mechanical mind in history*, 185–211.

Boden, M. A. (2004). *The creative mind: Myths and mechanisms*. Routledge.

Born, G. (1995). *Rationalizing culture: IRCAM, Boulez, and the institutionalization of the musical Avant-Garde*. University of California Press.

Bostrom, N. (2014). *Superintelligence: Paths, dangers, strategies* (1st ed.). Oxford University Press.

Breuer, H. P. (1975). Samuel Butler's "the book of the machines" and the argument from design. *Modern Philology*, *72*(4), 365–383.

Brown, T., Mann, B., Ryder, N., Subbiah, M., Kaplan, J. D., Dhariwal, P., Neelakantan, A., Shyam, P., Sastry, G., Askell, A., Agarwal, S., Herbert-Voss, A., Krueger, G., Henighan, T., Child, R., Ramesh, A., Ziegler, D. M., Wu, J., Winter, C., . . . Amodei, D. (2020). Language models are few-shot learners. *Advances in Neural Information Processing Systems*, *33*, 1877–1901.

Butler, S. (2015). *Erewhon and erewhon revisited*. Courier Dover Publications.

Cage, J. (1961). *Silence: Lectures and writings*. Wesleyan University Press.

Cardew, B. (2018, September 24). Ash Koosha: Return 0. *Pitchfork*. Retrieved August 5, 2022, from https://pitchfork.com/reviews/albums/ash-koosha-return-0/

Chung, S. (2018). Omnia per Omnia (2018)—Sougwen Chung (愫君). *Sougwen.com*. Retrieved August 9, 2022, from https://sougwen.com/project/omniaperomnia

Church, A. (1936). A note on the entscheidungsproblem. *The Journal of Symbolic Logic*, *1*(1), 40–41.

Cohen, H. (1982, December). How to make a drawing. In *Talk given to the science colloquium* (Vol. 17). National Bureau of Standards.

Colton, S. (2020). Possibilities and limitations for AI: What can't machines do? In R. Skidelsky & N. Craig (Eds.), *Work in the future: The automation revolution*. Springer Nature.

Cope, D. (1992). Computer modeling of musical intelligence in EMI. *Computer Music Journal*, *16*(2), 69–83.

Darville, J. (2020, December 16). Arca shares 100 different remixes of "Riquiquí" generated by A.I. *The Fader*. Retrieved August 5, 2022, from www.thefader.com/2020/12/16/arca-shares-100-different-remixes-of-riquiqu-generated-by-ai

Dhariwal, P., Jun, H., Payne, C., Kim, J. W., Radford, A., & Sutskever, I. (2020). Jukebox: A generative model for music. *arXiv preprint arXiv:2005.00341*.

Dhariwal, P., & Nichol, A. (2021). Diffusion models beat GANs on image synthesis. *Advances in Neural Information Processing Systems*, *34*, 8780–8794.

Dick, P. F. (1968). *Do androids dream of electric sleep?* Doubleday.

Dreyfus, H. L. (1965). *Alchemy and artificial intelligence*. RAND Corporation.

Dreyfus, H. L. (1976). What computers can't do. *British Journal for the Philosophy of Science*, *27*(2).

Dreyfus, H. L. (1992). *What computers still can't do: A critique of artificial reason*. MIT Press.

Eck, D., & Schmidhuber, J. (2002). *Finding temporal structure in music: Blues improvisation with LSTM recurrent networks*. IEEE Workshop on Neural Networks for Signal Processing.

El-Dabh, H. (1944). *Wire recorder piece* [composition]. https://classical20.com/2013/01/15/halim-el-dabh-wire-recorder-piece-1944/

Elgammal, A. (2019). AI is blurring the definition of artist: Advanced algorithms are using machine learning to create art autonomously. *American Scientist*, *107*(1), 18–22.

Ellison, H. (1967). I have no mouth, and i must scream. In *IF: Worlds of science fiction* (pp. 162–175). Galaxy Publishing Corp.

Engel, J., Hantrakul, L., Gu, C., & Roberts, A. (2020). *DDSP: Differentiable digital signal processing*. arXiv preprint arXiv:2001.04643. https://arxiv.org/abs/2001.04643

Esser, P., Rombach, R., & Ommer, B. (2021). Taming transformers for high-resolution image synthesis. In *Proceedings of the IEEE/CVF conference on computer vision and pattern recognition* (pp. 12873–12883). IEEE, CVF.

Fiebrink, R., Trueman, D., & Cook, P. R. (2009). *A meta-instrument for interactive, on-the-fly machine learning*. https://soundlab.cs.princeton.edu/publications/FiebrinkTruemanCook_NIME2009.pdf

Fjelland, R. (2020). Why general artificial intelligence will not be realized. *Humanities and Social Sciences Communications*, *7*(1), 1–9.

Flynn, M. (2018). A 19-year-old developed the code for the AI portrait that sold for $432,000 at Christie's. *Washington Post*, *26*.

Fry, A. (2021). EDM, meet AI. *The Evolution of Electronic Dance Music*, 81–102.

Gardner, H. (1987). *The mind's new science: A history of the cognitive revolution*. Basic Books.

Goodfellow, I., Pouget-Abadie, J., Mirza, M., Xu, B., Warde-Farley, D., Ozair, S., Courville, A., & Bengio, Y. (2014). Generative adversarial nets. *Advances in Neural Information Processing Systems*, *27*.

Google. (2022a, May). *Imagen*. Retrieved August 4, 2022, from https://imagen.research.google/

Google. (2022b, June). *Parti*. Retrieved August 4, 2022, from https://parti.research.google/

Harnad, S. (1990). The symbol grounding problem. *Physica D: Nonlinear Phenomena*, *42*(1–3), 335–346.

Hayles, K. N. (1999). *How we became Posthuman: Virtual bodies in cybernetics, literature, and informatics* (1st ed.). University of Chicago Press.

Heikkilä, M. (2023, March 21). How AI experts are using GPT-4. *MIT Technology Review*. https://www.technologyreview.com/2023/03/21/1070102/how-ai-experts-are-using-gpt-4/

Herndon, H. (2021, July 13). *Holly+*. Retrieved August 5, 2022, from https://holly.mirror.xyz/54ds2IiOnvthjGFkokFCoaI4EabytH9xjAYy1irHy94

Hiller, L. A., & Isaacson, L. M. (1957, October). Musical composition with a high speed digital computer. In *Audio engineering society convention 9*. Audio Engineering Society.

Jancer, M. (2018, May 17). More artists are writing songs in the key of AI. *Wired*. Retrieved August 5, 2022, from www.wired.com/story/music-written-by-artificial-intelligence/

Karras, T., Aittala, M., Laine, S., Härkönen, E., Hellsten, J., Lehtinen, J., & Aila, T. (2021). Alias-free generative adversarial networks. *Advances in Neural Information Processing Systems*, *34*, 852–863.

Kirn, P. (2020, July 6). Transfiguración: decolonizing AI, in Hexorcismos' shamanistic music and art - CDM Create Digital Music. *CDM Create Digital Music*. https://cdm.link/2020/07/transfiguracion-decolonizing-ai-in-hexorcismos-shamanistic-music-and-art/

Klingemann, M. (2017). *Imposture series* [visual art]. https://www.artsy.net/artwork/mario-klingemann-imposture-series-cobalamime

Kuivila, R. (2004). David Tutor: Live electronic music. *Leonardo Music Journal*, *14*, 106–107.

Kurzweil, R. (2005). *The singularity is near: When humans transcend biology*. Penguin.

Lattimore, R. (Ed.). (1894). *The Iliad of Homer*. Cambridge University Press.

Le Caine, H. (1955). *Dripsody: An étude for variable speed recorder* [composition]. NRC.

Lem, S. (2021). Lymphater's formula. In A. Lloyd-Jones (Ed.), *The truth and other stories* (pp. 221–248). MIT Press.

Lewis, G. E. (1996). Improvised music after 1950: Afrological and eurological perspectives. *Black Music Research Journal*, 91–122.

Lewis, G. E. (2000). Too many notes: Computers, complexity and culture in voyager. *Leonardo Music Journal*, *10*, 33–39.

Lewis, G. E. (2019). Listening for freedom with Arnold Davidson. *Critical Inquiry*, *45*(2), 434–447.

Lewis, G. E. (2021). Co-creation: Early steps and future prospects. In Bernard Lubat, Gérard Assayag, Marc Chemillier (Eds). Artisticiel / Cyber-Improvisations. Phonofaune, 2021, Dialogiques d'Uzeste., 2021. hal-03543133.

Lewis, J. P. (1988, July). Creation by refinement: A creativity paradigm for gradient descent learning networks. In *International conference on neural networks* (pp. 229–233). IEEE.

Linton, D. (1985). Luddism reconsidered. *ETC: A Review of General Semantics*, 32–36.

Maturana, H. R., & Varela, F. J. (1980). *Autopoiesis and cognition: The realization of the living (Boston studies in the philosophy and history of science, 42)* (1980th ed.). Springer.

Mayor, A. (2018). Gods and robots. In *Gods and robots*. Princeton University Press.

McCorduck, P. (1979). Machines Who Think: A Personal Inquiry into the History and Prospects of. *Intelligence*. San Francisco: Freeman.

McCulloch, W. S., & Pitts, W. (1943). A logical calculus of the ideas immanent in nervous activity. *The Bulletin of Mathematical Biophysics*, *5*(4), 115–133.

Mead, M. (1968). The cybernetics of cybernetics. In H. von Foerster, J. D. White, L. J. Peterson, & J. K. Russell (Eds.), *Purposive systems* (pp. 1–11). Spartan Books.

Midjourney. (2023, Mar). *Midjourney*. https://www.midjourney.com. Retrieved March 23, 2023, from https://www.midjourney.com

Miller, A. I. (2019). *The artist in the machine: The world of AI-powered creativity*. MIT Press.

Monahan, G. (1990). *Aeolian silo* [installation]. Funny Farm.

Nake, F. (2012). Construction and intuition: Creativity in early computer art. In *Computers and creativity* (pp. 61–94). Springer.

Oord, A. v. d., Dieleman, S., Zen, H., Simonyan, K., Vinyals, O., Graves, A., Kalchbrenner, N., Senior, A., & Kavukcuoglu, K. (2016). WaveNet: A generative model for raw audio. *Proceedings 9th ISCA Workshop on Speech Synthesis Workshop* (pp. 125–139).

OpenAI. (2021a, January). Dall-E 2. *OpenAI.com*. Retrieved August 4, 2022, from https://openai.com/dall-e-2/

OpenAI. (2021b, January). CLIP: Connecting text and images. *Openai.com*. Retrieved August 4, 2022, from https://openai.com/blog/clip/

Park, T., Liu, M. Y., Wang, T. C., & Zhu, J. Y. (2019). GauGAN: Semantic image synthesis with spatially adaptive normalization. In *ACM siggraph 2019 real-time live!* (p. 1). ACM.

Pask, G. (1969). *Colloquy of mobiles* [interactive art]. The ICA.

Payne, C. M. (2021, June 21). MuseNet. *OpenAI.com*. Retrieved August 4, 2022, from https://openai.com/blog/musenet/

Pein, C. (2018). *Live work work work die: A journey into the savage heart of silicon valley*. Metropolitan Books.

Petrič, Š. (2020). PL'AI. *Špela Petrič.org*. Retrieved August 8, 2022, from www.spelapetric.org/#/plai/

Polanyi, M. (1958). *Personal knowledge: Towards a post-critical philosophy* (1st ed.). University of Chicago Press.

Putnam, H. (1967). Psychological predicates. *Art, Mind, and Religion*, *1*, 37–48.

Quarshie, A. (2021, September 4). The quietus | features | a quietus interview | technology rewires your brain: Lee Gamble interviewed. *The Quietus*. Retrieved August 5, 2022, from https://thequietus.com/articles/30510-lee-gamble-interview

Raffel, C., Shazeer, N., Roberts, A., Lee, K., Narang, S., Matena, M., Zhou, Y., Li, W., & Liu, P. J. (2020). Exploring the limits of transfer learning with a unified text-to-text transformer. *Journal of Machine Learning Research*, *21*(140), 1–67.

Reich, S. (1965). *It's gonna rain* [composition]. https://en.wikipedia.org/wiki/It%27s_Gonna_Rain

Reichardt, J. (1968). *Cybernetic serendipity: The computer and the arts* (1st ed.). Studio International.

Reichardt, J. (1971). *Cybernetics, art and ideas*. Studio Vista.

Richey, J. L. (2011). I, robot. *Riding the Wind with Liezi: New Perspectives on the Daoist Classic, 193*.

Riskin, J. (2003). The defecating duck, or, the ambiguous origins of artificial life. *Critical inquiry*, *29*(4), 599–633.

Roberts, A. (2016). *The history of science fiction*. Palgrave Macmillan.

Roberts, A., Engel, J., Raffel, C., Hawthorne, C., & Eck, D. (2018, July). A hierarchical latent vector model for learning long-term structure in music. In *International conference on machine learning* (pp. 4364–4373). PMLR.

Roddy, S. (2017). Absolute nothingness—the Kyoto school and sound art practice. In R. Castro (Ed.), *Proceedings of the 2017 invisible places conference* (pp. 156–172). Invisible Places.

Roddy, S. (2023). Signal to noise loops: A cybernetic approach to musical performance with smart city data and generative music techniques. *Leonardo*, *56*(1).

Rombach, R., Blattmann, A., Lorenz, D., Esser, P., & Ommer, B. (2022). High-resolution image synthesis with latent diffusion models. In *Proceedings of the IEEE/CVF Conference on Computer Vision and Pattern Recognition* (pp. 10684–10695). IEEE, CVF.

Royal Northern College of Music. (2022, March 18). *George Lewis residency | RNCM musicians and an enhanced voyager—Royal Northern college of music*. RNCM. Retrieved

August 7, 2022, from www.rncm.ac.uk/research/research-centres-rncm/prism/prism-news/george-lewis-residency-rncm-musicians-and-an-enhanced-voyager/
Searle, J. R. (1980). Minds, brains, and programs. *Behavioral and Brain Sciences, 3*(3), 417–424.
Shanahan, M. (2015). *The technological singularity*. MIT Press.
Shannon, C. E. (1938). A symbolic analysis of relay and switching circuits. *Electrical Engineering, 57*(12), 713–723.
Sharkey, N. (2007). I ropebot. *New Scientist, 195*(2611), 32–35.
Sherburne, P. (2021, March 1). Mouse on mars: AAI. *Pitchfork*. Retrieved August 5, 2022, from https://pitchfork.com/reviews/albums/mouse-on-mars-aai/
Skidelsky, R. (2020). The future of work. In R. Skidelsky & N. Craig (Eds.), *Work in the future: The automation revolution*. Springer Nature.
SKYGGE. (2017). *Hello world album the first album composed with an artificial intelligence*. Retrieved August 4, 2022, from www.helloworldalbum.net/
Steadman, P. (2021). The automata of Hero of Alexandria. *Renaissance Fun: The Machines Behind the Scenes*, 111–132.
Steinbeck, P. (2018). George Lewis's voyager. In *The Routledge companion to jazz studies* (pp. 261–270). Routledge.
Todd, P. (1988). A sequential network design for musical applications. *Proceedings of the 1988 Connectionist Models Summer School*, 76–84.
Toffler, A. (1970). *Future shock*. Random House.
Tozer, T. (2020). What computers will never be able to do. In R. Skidelsky & N. Craig (Eds.), *Work in the future: The automation revolution*. Springer Nature.
Tudor, D. (1995). *Liner notes* [CD]. Lovely Music.
Turing, A. (1936). On computable numbers, with an application to the entscheidungsproblem. *Proceedings of the London Mathematical Society, 42*(1).
Tyka, M. (2018). *Portraits of imaginary people* [visual art]. https://www.interaliamag.org/audiovisual/mike-tyka/
Usselmann, R. (2003). The dilemma of media art: Cybernetic serendipity at the ICA London. *Leonardo, 36*(5), 389–396.
Various Artists. (1968). *Cybernetic serendipity music* [record]. Institute of Contemporary Arts.
Vinge, V. (1993). The coming technological singularity. *Whole Earth Review, 81*, 88–95.
von Foerster, H. (1984). *Observing systems*. Intersystems Publications.
von Neumann, J. (1945, June 30). *First draft of a report on the EDVAC* [Contract No. W]. https://en.wikipedia.org/wiki/First_Draft_of_a_Report_on_the_EDVAC
Warzel, C. (2023, February 8). Talking to AI might be the most important skill of this century. *The Atlantic*. https://www.theatlantic.com/technology/archive/2023/02/openai-text models-google-search-engine-bard-chatbot-chatgpt-prompt-writing/672991/
Wiener, N. (1948). *Cybernetics or control and communication in the animal and the machine*. MIT Press.
Woodcroft, B. (Ed.). (1851). *The pneumatics of Hero of Alexandria: From the original Greek*. Taylor, Walton and Maberly.
Xenakis, I. (1955). *Metastasis* [musical performance]. Donaueschingen Festival.
Xenakis, I. (1962). *Stratégie*. London: Boosey & Hawkes.
Young, L., & Zazeela, M. (1969). *Dream house* [installation]. https://en.wikipedia.org/wiki/Dream_House_(installation)
Zukowski, Z., & Carr, C. J. (2018). *Generating black metal and math rock: Beyond Bach, Beethoven, and Beatles*. arXiv preprint arXiv:1811.06639. https://scholar.google.com/citations?user=P7dSScMAAAAJ&hl=en

# 3 Slave to the 'Rithm

## The AI Turn in the Music Industries

*Sarah Keith, Steve Collins, Adrian Renzo and Alex Mesker*

### Introduction

The recent history of the music industries can be marked by several related themes concerned with particular technological interventions. These include the rise and effects of unauthorized file-sharing on the recorded music industry; the emergence of the digital "prosumer"; web 2.0 and social media practices; shifting concepts of labor and work; and the cultural and economic impact of music streaming.

An overview of music industry trade literature over the last few years reveals growing discussion of another technological intervention: artificial intelligence (AI) and related fields, including machine learning, data science and algorithmic processes. In "Music's Smart Future: How Will Artificial Intelligence Impact the Music Industry?," a 2016 report commissioned by the British Phonographic Industry, Geoff Taylor (BPI and BRIT Awards chief executive) asserted that AI is now "transforming how music is created, discovered, shared and enjoyed" (Ottewill, 2016). The potential of these technologies to be "the music industry's next Napster moment" (Dredge, 2021) is borne out by the increasing number of start-ups declaring AI as a core part of their operations and the growing attention paid to the topic by music industry trade publications. On the industry news site Music Business Worldwide, the number of articles mentioning "AI" in their title grew from one in 2018 to 17 in 2020. AI-driven platforms, services and applications are premised on the use of proprietary algorithms to improve or expedite necessary tasks within the music industries. For example, AI might analyze millions of songs to find the next "hit" or a track that is the perfect sync for a certain project; it might augment an artist's abilities by generating genre-appropriate musical accompaniment, or an entire song ex nihilo; or it might supply a "one-click" mix and master of a music track, applying signal processing chains derived from analyses of millions of preexisting songs. In a February 2020 symposium on AI held by the U.S. Copyright Office and the World Intellectual Property Organization (WIPO), David Hughes, Chief Technology Officer for the Recording Industry Association of America, voiced his concerns over the application of

DOI: 10.4324/9781003299875-3

AI to music, particularly the automation of music production: "Some of my close friends are audio engineers, and I'm not sure how this is going to impact their livelihoods. But hopefully they're old enough that they'll retire before they're all out of jobs" (United States Copyright Office, 2020, p. 186). This fatalistic description illustrates the profound effects AI is believed to have on the future music industries and their workers.

This chapter examines the "AI turn" within the music industries and considers the factors underlying the growth of interest in this area. We argue that this intervention should be considered not as the inexorable progress of technology but rather as an intentional product of the start-up economy, platform capitalism and technocratic thinking that has underpinned much of the early 21st century. The following discussion proposes the causes of recent AI-focused developments in the streaming-dominated musical ecosystem and considers what the increasing discourse around AI reveals about economic and technological changes to the music industries and their future. We argue that the present "AI moment" represents a re-consolidation of corporate power, where capital, knowledge and access lie increasingly in the hands of a few digital intermediaries and investors.

## A Brief Introduction to AI

The "AI turn" in the music industries did not emerge in a vacuum. In the first half of the 2010s, a number of scholars wrote about the "algorithmic turn" (after Uricchio, 2011) in the media industries. Referring to "the increasing prominence of algorithms in a variety of decision-making contexts," the "algorithmic turn" was a "response to growing quantities of available data, as well as a motivator for media organizations to gather ever more data from every available source to feed into massive processing capacities of these algorithms" (Napoli, 2014, p. 340). Algorithms redefine music as datasets: Snickars describes music as "the crude oil of our time waiting to be refined" (2016, p. 192), while Vonderau identifies "an economic belief in a conversion of values," a belief that data *about* music could be monetized (2015, p. 718). Algorithms promised to predict the next hits (Steiner, 2012, p. 86), generate new revenue streams through targeted advertisements and increase the quality of recommendation systems (Pham, 2014). Further developments expanded the potential of algorithms beyond prediction and into content creation (Napoli, 2014, p. 350). While algorithms and AI are closely related, AI has emerged as a distinct area of interest within the music industries. Despite the nebulous definition of AI as a technology, the increased use of the term establishes that "AI" possesses certain meanings and associations. If algorithms constitute technical processes like classification, recommendation and data management, then AI represents a supercharged network of algorithms, replicating or outperforming human-level creativity. In short, the algorithm defines a technical process, while AI signifies disruptive potential for capital gain. While the "algorithmic turn" is concerned with the implications of automated data collection and processing, the "AI turn" considers the broader economic and sectorial shifts causing, and resulting from, these changes.

The definition of artificial intelligence is inherently unstable. It is commonly associated (and conflated) with machine learning, an interdisciplinary field combining statistics, computer science, engineering and information theory to produce algorithms that "process data, make predictions, and help make decisions" (Jordan, 2019). Moore describes AI as "automating judgements that have previously been the exclusive domain of humans" (2019, p. 4), while Lipton argues the term is "aspirational, a moving target based on those capabilities that humans possess but which machines do not" (2018). AI's definition is therefore not only technical; it is dependent on context and the current state of the field. Crawford (in Simonite, 2021) goes further, proposing that AI is "neither artificial nor intelligent"; the term is used to obfuscate its human origins, materiality and political dimensions. Nonetheless, the term is a powerful indicator of prevailing neoliberal attitudes. AI "offers the entire business sector a shared narrative, a demonstrable vision of the future and a promise to 'jump start' the global economy through advanced technologies" (Bourne, 2019, p. 116). Positivist depictions of AI are generated through sustained public relations work on behalf of numerous vested interests: as Bourne notes, this is undertaken to create "unbridled enthusiasm for AI's potential as a capital-labour hybrid," "the 'perfect' model of efficiency" (p. 117). This promise has rendered AI a powerful term to stimulate investment interest. According to London-based venture capital firm MMC, however, 40% of European start-ups that claim to be using AI are, in fact, not (Olson, 2019). In the following discussion, we acknowledge the imprecise and contested definitions of "artificial intelligence." Nonetheless, its widespread use in popular discourse renders it a useful shorthand for data science, machine learning, algorithms and related processes.

## Outside Forces

It should come as no surprise that the application of AI to music has largely emerged from outside the music industries. The boundaries of the music industries are porous; new technologies and business models facilitate new entrants. This is not a 21st-century phenomenon; there is a long history of external forces injecting themselves into the music industries. As Harrington puts it, "technology threatens business as usual, until it becomes business as usual" (United States Copyright Office, 2020, p. 239).

The music industries comprise a myriad of activities relating to the production, consumption and distribution of music, many of which have been driven by the adoption of new technologies. Disruption is one of the defining characteristics of the music industries. For example, in the early 20th century, publishers' control over the printing and the performance of sheet music was challenged by the introduction of player pianos such as the pianola, which mechanically played songs according to instructions punched into rolls of paper. While piano rolls were effectively copies of songs, they were not considered copies for the purposes of the Copyright Act 1790. Consequently, producers of piano rolls had no legal obligation to compensate sheet music publishers for the use of their songs. The Copyright Act 1909 remedied this situation by creating a copyright in the composition of a song itself, thus requiring permission of the rights-holder if the song was reproduced in any format. Shortly after, the music industry was disrupted again by the introduction of recording technologies and then again by radio. Recordings rather than live performances (whether by actual musicians or mechanical players) became the dominant means to consume music. This shift affected how music itself was created. Performances still occurred, but the industry was reshaped around the practices and economies of record production: "The most important way of publicizing pop—the way most people heard most music—was on the radio, and records were made with radio formats and radio audiences in mind" (Frith, 1987, p. 62). Today, recordings remain the dominant way to consume music, and the recorded music industry depends on the streaming model founded on access rather than the sale of copies. The uptake of streaming models is the latest mark of a series of technological, economic, cultural and legislative changes (Collins et al., 2021a, p. 251).

These key changes (or "Napster moments") are frequently driven from outside the music industries. For example, the widespread shift toward music streaming was spearheaded by Spotify, which in 2006 was a tech start-up, but in 2021 is a key player in the music industries. There is a well-established pattern of technology companies moving into and becoming part of the music industries. Morris (2015, p. 21) recounts the long-standing "cross-pollination between the music industry and developers of new technologies (e.g. Edison cylinders, Berliner records, Philips and the audiotape, Sony/Philips and the CD)," adding that the "migration to digital music is unique in how tightly it has woven music and computing." Apple—a computer company—exemplified this principle when it released the iPod, established the iTunes Music Store and rapidly became a major entity in the music industries (Mnookin, 2007; Negus, 2019, p. 370). From Apple's foray into music onward, the deepest marks in the music industries have been cut by IT companies, which are "now the primary sector determining change" in music (Hesmondhalgh & Meier, 2018, p. 1556).

Software and IT companies now occupy pivotal roles across the gamut of music-related activities: in the context of music creation and production, the essential roles performed by digital audio workstations (DAWs), plugin instruments and effects, and audio interfaces have been further complemented by emergent cloud-based services proffering mixing, mastering, session musicians, sample libraries and AI-enhanced production. Music discovery, distribution and consumption have been reshaped by audio-identifying apps like

Shazam, platforms and intermediaries such as Bandcamp and Spotify, and compressed audio formats, portable devices and ubiquitous connectivity. Jonathan Sterne proposes:

> [M]edia industries scholars must [open] up our inquiries to a wide range of music industries; that is, industries whose activities directly affect the performance, production, circulation, consumption, recirculation, appropriation, and enjoyment of music today. Opening the term up in this way will allow us to develop more robust and coherent social accounts of music as a media practice, and provide a stronger empirical basis for criticizing current institutional arrangements and proposing new, more just and convivial alternatives.
>
> (Sterne, 2014, p. 50)

To understand the music industries in the 21st century is to move beyond the traditional and arguably outmoded constructs.

## Reasons for Interest in Music AI

Our central argument is that AI facilitates the data-enabled centralization of economic and cultural capital. We suggest that this centralization underpins much of the current interest in AI in the following five ways.

### *The Emergence of a Streaming Oligopoly*

Increasing music industry interest in AI is predicated on its capacity to generate revenue. This capacity requires the digitization of the music economy/ecology in order to extract meaningful and valuable data. Over the past decade, streaming has become the foremost means of music consumption and distribution, as well as the largest revenue sector for recorded music; the Recording Industry Association of America reports that total US music revenues from streaming have grown from 7% in 2010 (RIAA, 2015) to 83% in 2020 (RIAA, 2020).

This shift has yielded significant influence to a handful of intermediaries, notably Spotify. Although there are many music streaming services beyond the popular household names, the market is undoubtedly dominated by Spotify with its 31% share, followed at a distance by Apple Music, Amazon and China's Tencent at 15%, 13% and 13% respectively (Porter, 2022). One consequence is a "platformization of music curation [consisting] of a data-intense gatekeeping activity, based on different mixes of algo-torial logics, that produces new regimes of visibility" (Bonini & Gandini, 2019, p. 1). The obscured logics of this gatekeeping are informed by data, as well as arrangements of capital and rights; as Prey et al. (2020) discuss, the dependence of

Spotify on the three major labels, as both rights-holders and investors in the platform, incentivizes promotion of major label content over independent artists. A further effect is the growing aggregation of geographically distinct music sectors and markets, supplanting complex ecosystems of local, regional and national scenes, distributors, labels, retailers and radio stations. Although some geographical specificity is maintained by local playlists, these further centralize major platforms' reach over music practices and sectors. This consolidation is claimed to "propel artists to new heights and empower them to turn their passion into a profession [. . .] offering an unmatched catalog for [. . .] listeners" (Spotify, 2021a) but also minimizes some geographic specificity, such as policies designed to protect and support the production of local content (Morgan, 2020, p. 37). Increasing global availability is key to the platform logic of music streaming services; as Vonderau argues, the "seemingly boundless horizontal expansion of the music streaming market—more content, more users, more data, more ads" is necessary to build collateral value from songs and from audiences (2019, p. 15). A few music streaming services now administer the entire circulation of recorded music—global distribution, discovery and revenue generation—for an increasing number of users; data generated by users therefore presents a macrocosm of musical experience, presenting opportunities for algorithmic intervention by both streaming services themselves and third parties.

### *Music Datafication*

Digital platforms are data businesses by nature, necessarily automating processes such as classification, content filtering, tagging and recommendation in order to maintain and extract data/value from catalogues of (often user-generated) content, including text, audio, image and video. Platforms operate on a principle of data absorption, where "business units should be measured not just in terms of dollars absorbed but also in terms of monetizable data absorbed" (Choudhary, 2015, p. 41). This production of data is a hallmark of what Sadowski (2020) refers to as "rentier platforms," which coordinate and benefit from the acquisition, storage, analysis and valuation of data. Extracting data as "raw material" (Srnicek, 2017, p. 42) is a key function of platform capitalism; data is used to "educate and give competitive advantage to algorithms" (p. 33), which in turn generate new data for analysis. The focus on data has created new value for music; as Vonderau (2019, p. 15) observes, "music has become data, and data in turn has become contextual material for user targeting at scale." In turn, this has drawn the interest of digital conglomerates (such as Apple and Google) to music as a means to generate revenue-creating data (Negus, 2019, pp. 377–379). Music has therefore become a valuable commodity within the broader media and data industries, and AI is positioned as the key to effectively create and extract value from music in a streaming-dominated ecosystem.

As music's existence on streaming services is continually measured and quantified, the discernment of musical attributes, user habits, growth areas, trends and music listening practices is no longer reliant on "insider" or scene-specific knowledge but becomes a function of data. Tech start-ups have moved vigorously into this area. Analytics services such as Chartmetric and Sodatone provide forensic detail on radio play, streams and social media engagement. Observing, predicting and generating revenue from musical artefacts and user activities is an increasingly quantitative process. Specific musical expertise, from management to A&R, is thus partially ceded to data science, and this data feeds back into practice "in ways that feed-back, structure, delimit and even determine the circulations of popular culture" (Langley & Leyshon, 2017, p. 19). As Spotify's acquisition of music machine learning service the Echo Nest shows, streaming services also derive data from music itself, which is used, for example, to create automatic playlists of songs with similar attributes, thereby increasing user time on the service. Of particular relevance here is how the AI discourse represents an expansion of the datafied, algorithmic platform structure into areas deemed "creative" and services previously undertaken by human experts.

### *Music as Digital Asset*

Another factor underwriting the interest in musical AI is music's potential as a digital asset. Morris's (2015) thorough discussion of digital music commodities considers the material changes wrought by the transition from physical media to bought digital formats, and thenceforth to streaming subscriptions, pointing out the tension in "the classification of copies as commodities" (p. 179). Although labels and artists were initially "not convinced that the volume of new traffic [streaming] services generate [would] make up for the fact that consumers aren't paying $15 per CD," the success of catalogue licensing negotiations between rights-holders and streaming services indicates that cloud-based digital music subscriptions (and free, advertising-supported options) are considered profitable to both parties. This shift is due to recorded music's double status as copy *and* commodity. As an artifact with ownership and rights, digital music can be bought, sold and licensed as a commodity, but it can also be infinitely and economically provided to consumers as a copy. For streaming services, the profitability of digital music therefore consists of two related elements; zero-cost or low-cost content acquisition, and the infinite exploitation of digital goods by rights-holders.

In the current music industrial system, there is a marked asymmetry between top artists and the remainder of artists (Mulligan, 2014; Coelho & Mendes, 2019). Muikku (2017) enumerates this by surveying 10,000 randomly selected tracks on Spotify, revealing that 90% of tracks received fewer than 10 streams, and 0.4% of tracks received more than 100 streams (p. 9).

This unpaid productive labor by creators has hitherto been an under-considered subject of enquiry in the streaming economy; as Hesmondhalgh (2021) puts it, "a vast reserve army of cultural workers exists alongside a rather small group of professionals, a very select few of which gain huge financial rewards and fame" (p. 3602).

This system approaches what Fuchs (2011) calls the "infinite exploitation" of corporate web 2.0, where producers "work completely for free and are infinitely exploited" (p. 288). Producers (or, more accurately, rights-holders) are allocated a share of revenue, should their digital commodity be "sold," in the form of a stream, due to existing systems of music rights and royalty collection, but they are not paid for their initial labor, that is, their contribution to the catalogue. Srnicek (2017) identifies such businesses as *lean platforms*: "workers are outsourced, fixed capital is outsourced, maintenance costs are outsourced, and training is outsourced" (p. 53). In short, users—labels, producers and musicians—provide completed and saleable products at no direct cost to the platform (with the exception of licensing fees paid to major labels). The product for which streaming services' users are paying, in either attention or money—music—is not produced by the streaming service at all. The entire value created by such services lies in their centralization of user activity and the resulting extraction of data. As such, the value produced by streaming services is what Srnicek calls a "bare extractive minimum" (p. 53) produced by the platform's control over content, enabling it to collect a monopoly rent.

In many ways, music is the perfect digital commodity: it can be produced through immaterial labor and supplied for free by its creator; supply is plentiful due to the lowered (and still lowering) barriers to digital music production; a distribution infrastructure (including high-bandwidth telephony, digital compression protocols and mobile devices) is widely available, and its consumption is integrated into common day-to-day activities, whether commuting, working, exercising or sleeping. The wide availability of and audience for music in turn facilitates secondary generation of value through data, as discussed earlier; the millions of data points generated daily by music itself and the daily interactions of a platform's users (listeners, artists/labels, developers and advertisers) provide a macrocosm of the world of recorded music, an established economic sector in itself. In this space, AI serves as an alchemical interlocutor, finding "gold" among disparate and multiplying points of data and translating this value into revenue for extraction according to existing mechanisms of rights and royalties, synchronization, licensing and so on. For example, Snafu Records uses AI to comb through 150,000 songs a week in order to pass 15–20 over to its human A&R team (Millman, 2020). Similarly, Sodatone (which was acquired by Warner Music Group in 2018) uses machine learning to analyze artists' streaming, social media and touring data in an effort to profile and identify unsigned talent by early predictors of success (Warner Music Group, 2018).

### *Changing Musical Product Value*

The fourth reason underpinning increasing interest in AI for music is the declining economic value of recordings. The streaming economy has been a target for criticism by artists and other workers in the music industries for its low rates of payment, as shown by the UK Parliamentary inquiry in 2020 into the economics of music streaming (UK Parliament, 2021). Hubbs (2016) proposes that the mechanics of streaming have fundamentally changed music's perceived value, arguing that digital music "has the hallmark features of what economists call a public good, for digital music in a peer-to-peer network is neither a rivalrous nor an excludable good" (p. 136).

It is worth noting that the decommodification of recorded music did not originate from contemporary streaming services but rather from a set of circumstances in the mid-late 1990s: MP3s began spreading across the internet with Nullsoft's Winamp player helping to popularize the format. The uptake of this compressed format coincided with the emergence of broadband internet access and more affordable, large storage hard drives. Napster, *l'enfant terrible*, launched in 1999 and at its peak connected 25 million users to 80 million songs (Collins & Young, 2014, p. 56). The "celestial jukebox" eliminated "the inconvenience of thinking of music as a commodity" (Condry, 2004, p. 358). Although Napster—in its original incarnation—was short-lived, it triggered the emergence of a wave of similar peer-to-peer networks (such as Gnutella, eDonkey, LimeWire and Kazaa) that carried the same decommodifying message and initiated a battle for the control of music distribution. While alliances with technology companies like Apple helped forge a legitimate market for digital music, the "music is free" mindset never completely vanished as piracy still continues via peer-to-peer sharing, torrents, digital lockers and stream-ripping.

While Spotify can claim some responsibility for "turning the tide" (that is, drawing consumers to a legal alternative to piracy), the decommodification of music is built into its own service's relationship with its users. Music consumed via streaming lacks the intrinsic properties, and corresponding value, of private goods; it is more comparable to radio or a public library than a purchased commodity. Spotify founder Daniel Ek uses this reasoning in proposing that the monthly $10 rate for Spotify Premium is the upper limit of what consumers are willing to pay in an ecosystem that treats music as a public good, stating,

> You can go on radio and listen to [music], but you can also go on YouTube and you can find the entire archive of music including all the bootlegs and videos and you can listen to that entirely for free. That's what we're competing against.
>
> (Dubner, 2019)

Spotify's "Loud&Clear" website likewise rationalizes low per-stream rates as the only workable option, stating, "Raising prices is a fine balance—we don't want to drive people back to piracy or unmonetized solutions" (Spotify, 2021b). This "public good" conception of recorded music's value is promoted to refute the ongoing perception that streaming services offer unfairly low per-stream rates (Hesmondhalgh, 2021). The practice of stream-ripping—down loading content from streaming sites such as YouTube, thus removing it from circuits of surveillance and capital—has recently been identified as a growing threat (PRS For Music, 2020). Furthermore, Spotify's experimentation with lowering the stream rate further still in exchange for promotional consideration—a move that independent music company association IMPALA (2021) likens to payola—indicates that per-stream rates are unlikely to increase. Yet recorded music revenues have experienced six successive years of growth (IFPI, 2021, p. 11), with streaming revenues increasing almost 20% in 2019 alone (RIAA, 2019). The number of streaming service users and paying subscribers is likewise trending upward (Eliezer, 2020), resulting in increased cash inflow to these services as well as greater value created by the network effects of multiplying users (Srnicek, 2017, p. 32).

The competing headwinds of growing revenues across the recorded music sector as a whole, and low or diminishing per-stream returns for individual recordings, create an uncertain terrain for those seeking direct financial reward from recorded music. The existence of global territories and markets and the opacity of playlist curation and recommendation algorithms create further complexity. Data-driven solutions are proposed as the solution, for example, by services that find existing songs that are undervalued potential "hits" (Musiio, Instrumental) and those that automatically generate rights-free music (Mubert). As in all commercial enterprise, the underlying aim is to decrease costs and increase revenue. However, the window of profitability is shifting upward, requiring more listeners, more streams and more exposure, and simultaneously requiring lower costs of production. Commercial viability is therefore increasingly reliant on scalability.

### *Increased Participation*

The vast majority of digital music in streaming catalogues is the result of immaterial labor, produced by creators who receive little financial compensation for their contribution to the catalogue (and who, in fact, may be paying to contribute to the catalogue). Moreover, the number of creators is rising; the increasing capabilities of consumer technology, as well as high-bandwidth internet and powerful server-side processing have enabled a new market of "sub-amateur" (after Halter, 2009) music producers with little or no musical equipment or training, creating sample- and preset-driven music. Barriers to music production are low and still lowering, enabling creators to produce recordings with minimal outlay and at considerable speed. For example, Splice offers "Royalty-Free Sounds & Rent-to-Own Plugins" for $7.99 per month, while free-to-use apps like Voisey bring together beatmakers and singers and aim to "help people graduate from TikTok lip-sync wannabes to bona-fide songwriter/performers earning royalties" (Sparrow, 2020). A MIDiA research report proposes that the music industries are entering a "creator phase"—following on from a label phase, streaming phase and publisher phase—in which "creator tools companies become [the] subject of [an] investment gold rush" (Mulligan, 2021).

This shift to creators rests on several foundations: first, an expanding market sector of music creators, enabled by increasing access to technology; second, increasingly accessible networks of distribution, including social media and music-specific platforms, facilitating royalty collection and public exposure; third, creator tools are themselves reliant on algorithmic processes of filtering, categorization, ranking and data analysis. Voisey, for example, includes

> [an] algorithmic discovery system for three parties: singers who want to find a cool beat to perform over; users who want to find the hot new Voisey creations, and—crucially—the Voisey team and its partners, who are seeking that killer hook or breakout star.
>
> (Sparrow, 2020)

Other creator tools claiming to leverage algorithmic processes include the Trap Factory (n.d.) ("Have our AI generate beats for your next mixtape") and Loudly (2021) ("Our AI delivers infinite variations and limitless possibilities of song composition: new kinds of artists, new forms of music, new types of genres"). Similar plugins, applications and software as a service (SaaS) products exist for more specific areas of music production, such as iZotope's Neutron 3 Advanced, an "AI-powered mixing processor" (iZotope, 2019) and mastering (see Collins et al., 2021a, 2021b).

The emergence of these services reveals fundamental shifts within the music industries: music production is increasingly accessible, low-cost and subscription-based, facilitated by powerful and proprietary computational processes and therefore organized and centralized by applications, websites and services. AI forms an important part of these services' stated operations and public discourse to both users and investors, signaling data-driven insights, market competitiveness and scalability.

## Continuums of Technological Disruption

The 20th-century music industries still exist: recorded music, music publishing, live performance, music production, and their subsidiaries and satellites have adapted to profound changes over the last twenty-five years. How, then, is AI different from the many "disruptions" that have occurred in that time?

As outlined earlier, new services, applications and platforms that use (or claim to use) AI and algorithmic decision-making span the breadth of the music industries. The mass of information continually generated by streaming services, combined with increasing global accessibility of music, expanding participation in musical production, and low musical product value present a puzzle to which AI has been proposed as the answer. For artists, managers and other participants in the music industries today, not only *can* data be used, but it *must* be used to make sense of a complex and competitive music ecosystem. The music business today is therefore, increasingly, a data business. The following discussion outlines several points to argue this case.

Substantial investments are being made in music start-ups, and rights, often by venture capital and private equity firms outside (at least initially) the music or media industries. The economic value of music outside the music industries is well established; as Negus (2019, pp. 377–379) observes, digital conglomerates (such as Apple, Google and YouTube) have used music as a product that generates revenue-creating data. However, the increasing investment in music services and catalogues by venture capitalists is a newer development. The acquisition of sizable music catalogues by firms such as Hipgnosis is one recent trend; Hipgnosis itself is funded by both shareholders and New York-based investment firm Morgan Stanley (Ingham, 2021). The notion of music catalogues as a new investor asset class has been attributed to the finite number of "classic" songs, which, according to Hipgnosis founder Mark Mercuriadis, offer "predictable, reliable income" via streaming, syncs and covers (in Lynskey, 2021). However, investment in music rights relies on fundamental investment principles return on investment, earnings history and the like, which are informed by data. Royalty trading site Royalty Exchange directly links the increasing value of music catalogues to streaming and to data, stating,

> Collecting, aggregating and analyzing data has become much easier in the digital world, and royalty rightsholders [*sic*] are reaping the benefits. Better data means more accurate royalty collection and distribution, as well as easier analysis of music as an asset for investors.
>
> (Royalty Exchange, 2017)

This depiction of music as a data-rich investment property explains its attractiveness to venture capitalists: AI-driven trading is widely used in markets, and predictive analytic software is increasingly used by firms such as Goldman Sachs to efficiently manage assets (Mejia, 2020).

Likewise, music analytics services purporting to use AI to identify value in music have proliferated in the last five years. One example is Instrumental, an A&R scouting platform backed by venture capital firm Blenheim Chalcot, Warner Music UK and Tencent Music Entertainment Group (Stassen, 2020). Instrumental's stated mission is "to use AI and machine learning processes to discover high potential talent first and then offer the most compelling partnerships possible (across label, publishing, merchandising and licensing)"

(Instrumental, n.d.). According to founder Conrad Withey, Instrumental's algorithm includes "streaming performance including playlisting and follower growth, but also social engagement (broader popularity driven by sharing, subscribing etc)" (Ingham, 2020). Music analytics services, such as Soundcharts and Chartmetric, collate and present similar data; however, Instrumental adds an additional predictive function and is reportedly used by "all three major record companies—as well as a range of independent labels and entertainment industry heavyweights such as Live Nation" (Music Business Worldwide, 2018). Under this model, artists themselves—rather than recorded music rights—are presented as quantifiable investment properties. It is unlikely that the more "traditional" aspects of A&R, relying on specific scene, geographic and cultural expertise, will become completely obsolete; however, the foregrounding of data as evidence of potential is notable. An interview with Withey in *WIRED* discloses that "he's even signed musicians without having ever heard them" (Ralston, 2021); the same interview later states, "[W]hile Instrumental can find music that's popular, it's not always 'good'," Withey admits. Instrumental's proprietary processes are not open to scrutiny, and like other algorithmic interventions in recorded music, the means by which it calculates artist "value" or "potential" is both questionable and unknown. The long-term effect of AI- and data-driven A&R on the musical landscape may be profound; as Crawford (2021, p. 131) points out, pattern recognition produces "a statistical ouroboros," feeding data back into the system and amplifying inequalities in each iteration. AI therefore not only shapes the demand side of recorded music, by recommending certain tracks or artists to listeners on streaming platforms; it also shapes the supply aspect by nominating artists to scout, support and invest in and therefore the entire musical terrain.

The changes outlined earlier have yielded a highly competitive recorded music sector, facing an abundance of supply (i.e., increased participation), a finite market (i.e., limitations to listenership and the maturation of streaming as a format) and low per-stream revenue. One means of negotiating this challenging economic landscape is through data-driven analysis of tracks and artists, using methods adopted from finance, and specifically Fintech, to assess the value of musical properties and determine how to efficiently manage and exploit them. The other means is to address the "input" side of the equation, developing assistive creator tools for a growing market of amateur music producers. Both of these approaches entail treating music—including recordings, engagement, artists and composition—as data, and furthermore, using AI and related technologies to derive meaningful results from that data.

## Conclusion

Sterne (2014, p. 53) has rightly argued that there is no singular music industry but rather, "many industries with many relationships to music." Nonetheless the term is useful to describe established institutions and sectors, which have historically administered the circulation of recorded and performed music; its production, composition, rights, management and so on. These "old" music industries relied on specific technical knowledge, networks and structures of power and capital; these in turn were gate-kept by music producers, distributors, A&R personnel, managers, label heads and the like. Others (e.g., Hesmondhalgh & Meier, 2018; Negus, 2019; Prey et al., 2020) have since discussed the profound effects of streaming on these music industries, including both economic changes and growing incursions by information technology, data and (tele)communications sectors. The result of this shift is that musical practices are increasingly treated as data. Crawford (2021) attributes this change to "the emergence of a logic that has now thoroughly pervaded the tech sector: the unswerving belief that everything is data and is there for the taking" (p. 93).

Algorithmic interventions in music creation, curation and categorization have been widely discussed in recent years (see Morris, 2015; Lange, 2016; Bonini & Gandini, 2019). The consolidation of music discovery and consumption by streaming services positions AI as the next stage of development, integrating and leveraging previously distinct sectors to create a frictionless landscape enabled by the reduction of musical artifacts, practices and culture to data. Describing this connective function, Engster and Moore (2020) define AI as "the machine to socialise all other machines [. . .] socialising all the technical calculation machines already in force, but till [*sic*] today 'only' connected as single machines with no internal communication, no self-and deep-learning competence" (p. 214–215). Services purporting to use AI quantify and connect previously distinct sectors and areas, such as A&R and listener data, music composition and livestreaming, music listening and gaming, or music production and distribution. These connective functions are proposed as a new way to extract value from music, as the value of the individual music commodity diminishes, and the sociocultural and labor dimensions of music become obscured by data.

Although ethical and creative concerns over AI are worthy avenues of inquiry, this chapter argues that its implementation must also consider which parties and sectors stand to materially benefit from its use. The fundamental aim of musical AI is to render creative, aesthetic and subjective qualities as data. This in turn reduces the need for social and knowledge capital held by those within the music industries and opens music up to new "outsiders"—particularly venture capitalists and the finance sector—who are able to treat it as a transparent and quantified commodity. The increasing interest in AI for music is therefore predicated on this disruptive potential, and more precisely, its potential to radically reshape structures of power and capital to serve certain intermediaries and interests. Beneficiaries of this landscape include scale-focused platforms, investors, rights-holders of substantial catalogues (and their investors), while smaller actors and individuals are "squeezed out." While prevailing corporate discourse on AI emphasizes its democratizing aspect, we argue here that the AI "gold rush" is a rush to concentrate capital, knowledge and access for the benefit of a small number of digital intermediaries and investors.

## References

Bonini, T., & Gandini, A. (2019). "First week is editorial, second week is algorithmic": Platform gatekeepers and the platformization of music curation. *Social Media + Society*, *5*(4), 1–11. https://doi.org/10.1177/2056305119880006

Bourne, C. (2019). AI cheerleaders: Public relations, neoliberalism and artificial intelligence. *Public Relations Inquiry*, *8*(2), 109–125. https://doi.org/10.1177/2046147X19835250

Choudhary, S. P. (2015). *Platform scale: How a new breed of startups is building large empires with minimal investment*. Platform Thinking Labs Pvt. Ltd.

Coelho, M. P., & Mendes, J. Z. (2019). Digital music and the "death of the long tail." *Journal of Business Research*, *101*, 454–460. https://doi.org/10.1016/j.jbusres.2019.01.015

Collins, S., Renzo, A., Keith, S., & Mesker, A. (2021a). Transformations and continuities in the mastering sector. In J. P. Braddock, R. Hepworth-Sawyer, J. Hodgson, M. Shelvock, & R. Toulson (Eds.), *Mastering in music* (pp. 249–263). Routledge.

Collins, S., Renzo, A., Keith, S., & Mesker, A. (2021b). Mastering 2.0: The real or perceived threat of DIY mastering and automated mastering systems. *Popular Music and Society*, *44*(3), 258–273. https://doi.org/10.1080/03007766.2019.1699339

Collins, S., & Young, S. (2014). *Beyond 2.0: The future of music*. Equinox.

Condry, I. (2004). Cultures of music piracy: An ethnographic comparison of the US and Japan. *International Journal of Cultural Studies*, *7*(3), 343–363. https://doi.org/10.1177/1367877904046412

Crawford, K. (2021). *Atlas of AI: Power, politics, and the planetary costs of artificial intelligence*. Yale University Press.

Dredge, S. (2021, April 27). Plastikman and Endel talk AI music: "This is uncharted territory." *Musically*. Retrieved June 4, 2021, from https://musically.com/2021/04/27/plastikman-and-endel-talk-ai-music-this-is-uncharted-territory/

Dubner, S. J. (Host). (2019, April 10). How Spotify saved the music industry (but not necessarily musicians) (No. 374) [Audio podcast episode]. In *Freakonomics*. Renbud Radio, LLC. https://freakonomics.com/podcast/how-spotify-saved-the-music-industry-but-not-necessarily-musicians-ep-374/

Eliezer, C. (2020, November 2). Spotify, Apple and YouTube music enjoy revenue, subscriber boosts. *The Music Network*. Retrieved April 22, 2021, from https://themusicnetwork.com/spotify-apple-youtube-music-revenue-q2-2020/

Engster, F., & Moore, P. V. (2020). The search for (artificial) intelligence, in capitalism. *Capital and Class*, *44*(2), 201–218. https://doi.org/10.1177/0309816820902055

Frith, S. (1987). The industrialization of popular music. In J. Lull (Ed.), *Popular music and communication* (pp. 53–77). Sage.

Fuchs, C. (2011). *Foundations of critical media and information studies*. Routledge.

Halter, E. (2009, April 29). After the Amateur: Notes. *Rhizome*. Retrieved April 3, 2021, from https://rhizome.org/editorial/2009/apr/29/after-the-amateur-notes/

Hesmondhalgh, D. (2021). Is music streaming bad for musicians? Problems of evidence and argument. *New Media and Society*, *23*(12), 3593–3615. https://doi.org/10.1177/1461444820953541

Hesmondhalgh, D., & Meier, L. M. (2018). What the digitalisation of music tells us about capitalism, culture and the power of the information technology sector. *Information, Communication & Society*, *21*(11), 1555–1570. https://doi.org/10.1080/1369118X.2017.1340498

Hubbs, G. (2016). Digital music and public goods. In R. Purcell & R. Randall (Eds.), *21st century perspectives on music, technology, and culture: Listening spaces* (pp. 134–152). Palgrave Macmillan.

IFPI (International Federation of the Phonographic Industry). (2021, March). *Global music report 2021*. IFPI. Retrieved June 18, 2021, from https://gmr2021.ifpi.org/assets/GMR2021_State%20of%20the%20Industry.pdf

IMPALA (Independent Music Companies Association). (2021, March). *It's time to challenge the flow: How to make the most of the real opportunities of streaming*. IMPALA. Retrieved April 12, 2021, from https://impalamusic.org/wp-content/uploads/2021/03/IMPALA-streaming-ten-point-plan-March-2021.pdf

Ingham, T. (2020, June 22). Conrad Withey, instrumental: "This generation of artists are savvy about their own potential, rights and commercial worth." *Music Business Worldwide*. Retrieved February 25, 2020, from www.musicbusinessworldwide.com/this-generation-of-artists-are-savvy-about-their-own-potential-rights-and-commercial-worth/

Ingham, T. (2021, February 5). Hipgnosis raises another $100M . . . led by Morgan Stanley money. *Music Business Worldwide*. Retrieved June 20, 2021, from www.musicbusinessworldwide.com/hipgnosis-raises-another-100m-led-by-morgan-stanley-money/

Instrumental. (n.d.). About us. *Instrumental*. Retrieved June 20, 2021, from www.weareinstrumental.com/about

iZotope. (2019, June 6). What's new in neutron 3? *iZotope*. Retrieved June 20, 2021, from www.izotope.com/en/learn/whats-new-in-neutron-3.html

Jordan, M. I. (2019). Artificial intelligence—the revolution hasn't happened yet. *Harvard Data Science Review*, *1*(1). https://doi.org/10.1162/99608f92.f06c6e61

Lange, B. (2016). The evolution of music tastemakers in the digital age: The rise of algorithms and the response of journalists. In B. J. Hracs, M. Seman, & T. E. Virani (Eds.), *The production and consumption of music in the digital age* (pp. 237–247). Routledge.

Langley, P., & Leyshon, A. (2017). Platform capitalism: The intermediation and capitalization of digital economic circulation. *Finance and Society*, *3*(1), 11–31. https://doi.org/10.2218/finsoc.v3i1.1936

Lipton, Z. C. (2018, June 5). From AI to ML to AI: On swirling nomenclature & slurried thought. *Approximately Correct*. Retrieved April 16, 2021, from http://approximatelycorrect.com/2018/06/05/ai-ml-ai-swirling-nomenclature-slurried-thought/

Loudly. (2021). Music AI. *Loudly*. Retrieved June 20, 2021, from www.loudly.com/aimusicstudio/

Lynskey, D. (2021, February 27). "Record companies have me on a dartboard": The man making millions buying classic hits. *The Guardian*. Retrieved June 20, 2021, from www.theguardian.com/music/2021/feb/27/merck-mercuriadis-the-man-who-is-shaking-up-the-music-industry

Mejia, N. (2020, March 18). Artificial intelligence at Goldman Sachs—current initiatives. *Emerj*. Retrieved June 20, 2021, from https://emerj.com/ai-sector-overviews/artificial-intelligence-goldman-sachs/

Millman, E. (2020, February 13). This new record label is using an algorithm to find its artists. *Rolling Stone*. Retrieved June 20, 2021, from www.rollingstone.com/pro/features/snafu-records-launches-with-artificial-intelligence-948212/

Mnookin, S. (2007, November 27). Universal's CEO once called iPod users thieves: Now he's giving songs away. *Wired*. Retrieved June 20, 2021, from www.wired.com/2007/11/mf-morris/

Moore, A. (2019, June 7). When AI becomes an everyday technology. *Harvard Business Review*. Retrieved June 19, 2021, from https://hbr.org/2019/06/when-ai-becomes-an-everyday-technology

Morgan, B. A. (2020). Revenue, access, and engagement via the in-house curated Spotify playlist in Australia. *Popular Communication, 18*(1), 32–47. https://doi.org/10.1080/15405702.2019.1649678

Morris, J. W. (2015). *Selling digital music, formatting culture*. University of California Press.

Muikku, J. (2017, November 30). *Pro rata and user centric distribution models: A comparative study*. Digital Media Finland. Retrieved June 20, 2021, from www.digitalmedia.fi/wp-content/uploads/2018/02/UC_report_final_171213.pdf

Mulligan, M. (2014, July 14). *The death of the long tail? The superstar music economy*. MIDiA. Retrieved June 17, 2021, from www.midiaresearch.com/reports/the-death-of-the-long-tail

Mulligan, M. (2021, April 16). *The music industry's centre of gravity is shifting*. MIDiA. Retrieved June 17, 2021, from www.midiaresearch.com/blog/the-music-industrys-centre-of-gravity-is-shifting

Music Business Worldwide. (2018, July 25). A&R scouting platform instrumental strikes deal with UK's official charts company. *Music Business Worldwide*. Retrieved June 20, 2021, from www.musicbusinessworldwide.com/ar-scouting-platform-instrumental-strikes-deal-with-uks-official-charts-company/

Napoli, P. M. (2014). Automated media: An institutional theory perspective on algorithmic media production and consumption. *Communication Theory, 24*(3), 340–360. https://doi.org/10.1111/comt.12039

Negus, K. (2019). From creator to data: The post-record music industry and the digital conglomerates. *Media, Culture and Society, 41*(3), 367–384. https://doi.org/10.1177/0163443718799395

Olson, P. (2019, March 4). Nearly half of all "AI startups" are cashing in on hype. *Forbes*. Retrieved June 17, 2021, from www.forbes.com/sites/parmyolson/2019/03/04/nearly-half-of-all-ai-startups-are-cashing-in-on-hype/

Ottewill, J. (2016, November 24). New BPI report reveals how AI is impacting the music industry. *PRS for Music*. Retrieved June 20, 2021, from www.prsformusic.com/m-magazine/news/new-bpi-report-reveals-ai-impacting-music-industry

Pham, A. (2014, June 3). *Business matters: Why Spotify bought the echo nest*. Billboard. Retrieved July 23, 2021, from https://assets.billboard.com/articles//5930133/business-matters-why-spotify-bought-the-echo-nest

Porter, J. (2022, January 20). Streaming music report sheds light on battle between Spotify, Amazon, Apple, and Google. *The Verge*. Retrieved April 20, 2022, from www.theverge.com/2022/1/20/22892939/music-streaming-services-market-share-q2-2021-spotify-apple-amazon-tencent-youtube

Prey, R., Esteve Del Valle, M., & Zwerwer, L. (2020). Platform pop: Disentangling Spotify's intermediary role in the music industry. *Information, Communication & Society*, *25*(1), 74–92. https://doi.org/10.1080/1369118X.2020.1761859

PRS for Music. (2020, September). Stream-ripping: Its role in the UK music piracy landscape three years on. *PRS for Music*. Retrieved June 20, 2021, from www.prsformusic.com/-/media/files/prs-for-music/research/full-stream-ripping-research-report-2020.pdf

Ralston, W. (2021, April 30). This startup finds the music megastars of the future. *Wired*. Retrieved June 20, 2021, from www.wired.co.uk/article/instrumental-music-talent

RIAA (Recording Industry Association of America). (2015). News and notes on 2015 RIAA shipment and revenue statistics. *RIAA*. Retrieved June 20, 2021, from www.riaa.com/wp-content/uploads/2016/03/RIAA-2015-Year-End-shipments-memo.pdf

RIAA (Recording Industry Association of America). (2019). Year-end 2019 RIAA revenue statistics. *RIAA*. Retrieved June 20, 2021, from www.riaa.com/wp-content/uploads/2020/02/RIAA-2019-Year-End-Music-Industry-Revenue-Report.pdf

RIAA (Recording Industry Association of America). (2020). Year-end 2020 RIAA revenue statistics. *RIAA*. Retrieved June 20, 2021, from www.riaa.com/wp-content/uploads/2021/02/2020-Year-End-Music-Industry-Revenue-Report.pdf

Royalty Exchange. (2017, November 10). Why music royalties belong in your portfolio. *Royalty Exchange*. Retrieved June 20, 2021, from www.royaltyexchange.com/blog/why-music-royalties-belong-in-your-portfolio

Sadowski, J. (2020). The internet of landlords: Digital platforms and new mechanisms of rentier capitalism. *Antipode: A Radical Journal of Geography*, *52*(2), 562–580. https://doi.org/10.1111/anti.12595

Simonite, T. (2021, April 26). This Researcher Says AI Is Neither Artificial nor Intelligent. *Wired*. Retrieved June 20, 2021, from www.wired.com/story/researcher-says-ai-not-artificial-intelligent/

Snickars, P. (2016). More music is better music. In P. Wikström & R. DeFillip (Eds.), *Business innovation and disruption in the music industry* (pp. 191–210). Edward Elgar.

Sparrow, J. (2020, January 27). Music ally startup files: Voisey is the TikTok for music creation. *Musically*. Retrieved June 19, 2021, from https://musically.com/2020/01/27/music-ally-startup-files-voisey-is-the-tiktok-for-music-creation/

Spotify. (2021a, February 22). Spotify expands international footprint, bringing audio to 80+ new markets. *Spotify Newsroom*. Retrieved June 20, 2021, from https://newsroom.spotify.com/2021-02-22/spotify-expands-international-footprint-bringing-audio-to-80-new-markets/

Spotify. (2021b). Why doesn't Spotify just charge listeners more? *Loud&Clear*. Retrieved June 20, 2021, from https://loudandclear.byspotify.com/?question=spotify-pricing

Srnicek, N. (2017). *Platform capitalism*. Polity Press.

Stassen, M. (2020, October 28). Tencent confirms buying minority stake in AI-driven A&R platform instrumental. *Music Business Worldwide*. Retrieved June 20, 2021, from www.musicbusinessworldwide.com/tencent-confirms-taking-minority-stake-in-ai-driven-ar-platform-instrumental/

Steiner, C. (2012). *Automate this: How algorithms came to rule our world*. Portfolio, Penguin.

Sterne, J. (2014). There is no music industry. *Media Industries Journal*, *1*(1), 50–55. https://doi.org/10.3998/mij.15031809.0001.110

The Trap Factory. (n.d.). *The trap factory*. Retrieved June 20, 2021, from https://thetrapfactory.com

UK Parliament. (2021, July 15). *Economics of music streaming inquiry*. Retrieved June 20, 2021, from https://committees.parliament.uk/work/646/economics-of-music-streaming

United States Copyright Office. (2020, February 5). *Copyright in the age of artificial intelligence (transcript)*. Retrieved June 20, 2021, from www.copyright.gov/events/artificial-intelligence/transcript.pdf

Uricchio, W. (2011). The algorithmic turn: Photosynth, augmented reality and the changing implications of the image. *Visual Studies*, *26*(1), 25–35. https://doi.org/10.1080/1472586X.2011.548486

Vonderau, P. (2015). The politics of content aggregation. *Television & New Media*, *16*(8), 717–733. https://doi.org/10.1177/1527476414554402

Vonderau, P. (2019). The Spotify effect: Digital distribution and financial growth. *Television & New Media*, *20*(1), 3–19. https://doi.org/10.1177/1527476417741200

Warner Music Group. (2018, March 28). Warner music group acquires sodatone. *Warner Music Group*. Retrieved June 20, 2021, from www.wmg.com/news/warner-music-group-acquires-sodatone-33396

# 4 A "New Economy" of Blockbusters?

## Netflix, Algorithms and the Narratives of Transformation in Audiovisual Capitalism

*Christophe Magis*

Lockdown measures imposed by most governments in the face of the COVID-19 pandemic have undoubtedly had a major impact on the cinema and audiovisual economy. For the past two years, this is at least what Hollywood analysts have repeated: with movie theaters closed, studios were deprived of their main outlet, leading to an accelerated transformation of the sector. Some, like Metro-Goldwin-Mayer, were able to postpone the release of the latest James Bond for over a year. For their part, most of the smaller producers were forced to turn to subscription video on demand (SVOD) platforms. This was even the choice made by a major like Warner (acquired by telecommunication giant AT&T in 2016), which decided, in addition to postponing films such as Denis Villeneuve's *Dune* by almost a year, to release it simultaneously in theaters and on its streaming service HBO Max to the bitter dissatisfaction of the director.[1]

Disrupting the traditional routines of the film industry, such strategic choices in response to the pandemic have shifted some of the economic stakes of the sector, with various repercussions. The suit filed in July 2021 by the actress Scarlett Johansson against Disney concerning her fee for appearing in *Black Widow* is worth noting. This superhero movie was programmed for release in the spring of 2020, but this was pushed back to the summer of 2021, both in cinemas and on the Disney+ platform. However, in line with the usual mode of remuneration for movie stars, Johansson's contract indexed part of her fee to box office returns, making the period of theatrical release before streaming platform availability extremely important. While an arrangement was finally reached by fall 2021, it is interesting to note how the pandemic itself was at the heart of Disney's defense of its transformation of the traditional media chronology. On a less dramatic level, the post-pandemic context was, moreover, at the heart of hard-fought negotiations between the International

1 "Dune" director Denis Villeneuve blasts HBO max deal. (2020, December 10). *Variety*.

DOI: 10.4324/9781003299875-4

Alliance of Stage, Theater and Film Employees (IATSE, a major American movie-workers union) and the studios for better remuneration of creative workers. In short, as *The Economist* put it at the end of 2021, it seems that "the pandemic is reshaping which films are made and where they are viewed" creating a "tense social climate": "it is a turbulent time in Tinseltown"![2]

At the center of this turbulence were the SVOD algorithms and their analysis of user preferences, presented as being the actual driving force behind the radical transformation of the audiovisual sector, which the pandemic merely accelerated. Since the beginning of the last decade, big data analysis has supposedly been able to determine which actors are likely to generate significant returns on investment in films and which actors are overpaid. The UK-based company Epagogix (created in 2003) even uses an algorithm to advise studios on the choice of actors and plots.[3] With the rise of Netflix and its success in commissioning original content, algorithms have increasingly been present in the debate on changes in the audiovisual economy. They have become a topic for industry conferences and trade publications, as well as in the specialized press and lately in academic discussion. The dominant discourse is that algorithm-based recommendation systems tend to free online content providers from reliance on stars and on the uncertain search for hit movies and blockbusters (Finn, 2017; Uricchio, 2017). Stars and blockbusters are no longer, in this view, so necessary in the risk-attenuation strategies of the film industry, since algorithmic data knows better what movies to make, for what kind of audiences and how to amplify successes, allowing more money to be spent on fewer films—but of much better quality.

This chapter analyzes the argument that recommendation algorithms are profoundly transforming the audiovisual economy, paving the way for a "new economics of blockbusters."[4] To this end, we will focus on the socioeconomic strategies of Netflix since its entry into content production. As we will see, while the idea of cultural production guided by algorithms is becoming widespread, actual strategies tend to be closer to the traditional functioning of the audiovisual industry. Therefore, a more theory-oriented discussion will aim at understanding cultural algorithms as a *myth* accompanying the deployment of capitalism in the media.

## The Question of Uncertainty in the Transformation of the Audiovisual Industries

Firstly, an important theoretical reminder. Research carried out on the cultural industries reveals that cultural and media products all share a main common

2 How Hollywood's biggest stars are losing their clout. (2021, November 8). *The Economist*.

3 Slaves to the algorithm. (2013, December 31). *The Economist*.

4 The new economics of blockbusters. (2021, March 13). *The Economist*.

socioeconomic feature: their valorization is highly uncertain. As the use-values of these products are "difficult if not impossible to pin down in any precise terms, the demand for them appears to be similarly volatile" (Garnham, 1990, p. 161). Cultural production is therefore a "risky business" (Prindle, 1993), where "fashionable performers or styles, even if heavily marketed, can suddenly come to be perceived as outmoded and, equally, other texts can become unexpectedly successful" (Hesmondhalgh, 2013, p. 19). Consequently, throughout the history of this sector, profits depend on highly unpredictable factors. And since, at the same time, investors tend to have a high degree of risk aversion, the question of uncertainty is at the core of certain research perspectives. For instance, the methodological "modelization" principle developed by the French "cultural industries" school draws upon the analysis of this distinctive feature (Mœglin, 2007).

In the film industry in particular, different eras are traditionally named after the strategies put in place to cope with uncertainty. Indeed, what is usually referred to as Hollywood's "studio-system" in its "golden" or "classic" era—opposed to a later "star-system" or "New Hollywood" era—was first and foremost a reorganization of the production process to manage the risk inherent to the cultural sector, characterized by dense vertical integration: the studios intervened at every stage of production, and planned and standardized its every facet (Balio, 1976). By the late 1920s and until the early 1950s, the sector was dominated by a handful of major studios who

> not only made motion pictures, but they also leased them through their own distribution companies to theaters which they themselves controlled. Although the "majors"—along with significant "minors" like Columbia, Universal-International Republic, and Monogram—never controlled more than one sixth of the movie theaters in the United States, they did control most of the important "first run" houses.
>
> (Schatz, 1981, p. 4)

This oligopoly of companies could then assure market domination through practices such as *block-booking* (forcing exhibitors to accept bundles of films, few of which were explicitly sought after), *blind-bidding* (exhibitors normally had no opportunity to watch films before bidding on a bundle) or admission price fixing. These tactics were ways of limiting the risk by ensuring the circulation of products when directors and actors were under contract to studios (Chapman, 2003).

Antitrust laws were implemented at the turn of the 1950s, notably after the Paramount Case of 1948, which led to the vertical disintegration of the sector and marked the end of existing trade practices. This led to other strategies to cope with risk. This "New Hollywood era" is usually called "the star system" following the new role that star actors came to play. No longer tied to the studios, actors and directors were able to choose their projects, leading to a handful of superstars who, having achieved recognition for their acting or directing ability as much as for the quality of their films, could maximize a movie's chances of success just by being involved with it. Stars have since been used by studios to limit the risk of failure and assure audience maximization in the case of success within a "catalogue strategy" in which productors "offset misses against hits by means of 'overproduction'" (Hesmondhalgh, 2013, p. 22). Furthermore, studios have progressively increased spending on stars and marketing for "blockbusters" earmarked for success.

For its part, television follows another logic, coping with risk by organizing content into a coherent flow of scheduled programs, financed indirectly, either by specific levies (Williams, 1974; Flichy, 1980) or by the sale of viewing time to advertising companies (Smythe, 1977). In the schedule, "blockbusters" take their place alongside news bulletins, variety shows and so on in order to attract viewers at specific times. These programs can be produced by the network or purchased from external producers. Furthermore, especially in the case of commercial television, large quantities of socio-demographic data are used to correlate viewer types to specific programs in order to maximize the efficiency of advertising spots (Meehan, 1984). The progressive rise of Pay TV in the 1990s, relying on advertising revenues as well as on subscription or pay-per-view, has gradually shifted the ways risk is dealt with in television by offering large inventories of premium or niche programs virtually accessible through communication technologies (Lacroix & Tremblay, 1997).

It should also be added that deregulation measures were encouraged by neoliberal policies, from the late 1980s onward, leading to intense concentration in the media sector and especially in audiovisual production.

> Since then, the major film corporations have become part of enormous vertically integrated entertainment conglomerates that now own not only the major television networks, but also cable networks, video stores, and (some) theaters, as well as producing and distributing entertainment commodities for these outlets.
>
> (Wasko, 2005, p. 14)

This has led to ever-increasing production costs for films with intensive use of stars within global marketing strategies for the maximization of blockbuster audiences in a variety of media. These high costs operate as another way of attenuating risk by raising significant barriers to entry into the sector, hence limiting competition.

## Netflix's Trajectory: "Disruption," Algorithms and Ambitious Content . . .

These traditional risk management strategies with their heavy reliance on stars and blockbusters are supposedly being "disrupted," according to commentaries on the rise of SVOD services. This is particularly visible in the narratives surrounding the emergence and consolidation of Netflix.

Research on Netflix has shown how articles in the general as well as the specialized press have usually compared the corporation with a more traditional studio like Disney, even exaggerating the confrontation between the two. As Lucien Perticoz (2019, §10) indicates in a study covering the French economic press, these companies "are presented, on the one hand, as one of the most eminent representatives of the Hollywood industry and, on the other, as one of the jewels of Silicon Valley and the 'new economy'." Furthermore, Netflix is also compared with television channels like HBO[5]—following the comparison offered by Netflix's CEO himself—or the BBC.[6] Indeed, since the "new economy" emerged in the late 1990s, declaring that technologies (and especially digital devices and the internet) were to become increasingly important in restructuring the economy, every company or "*start-up*" seeking to technologically alter ways of doing business in any sector has been said to be "disruptive" and compared with traditional giant actors of this sector. In Netflix's case, these discourses even add some drama, in the light of the history of the company that started in 1997 as a DVD mail delivery service (transforming the film rental business) to become an audiovisual streaming subscription service leader and a content producer.[7] The company could then be presented as having undergone significant changes, such as the shift toward a subscription model for unlimited rentals, the introduction of a streaming service and its entry into producing content (Tryon, 2015). Therefore, Reed Hastings, Netflix's CEO, is usually praised for his "uncanny foresight," without which "Netflix would not be where it is."[8] For example, in a portrait published in *Fortune* in 2010, one reads:

> Hastings anticipated, virtually from the moment he started Netflix, that consumers would eventually prefer to get movies instantly delivered via the Internet. (Hastings' foresight is amazing, considering that back in 2000, less than 7% of U.S. homes had broadband.) And so rather than let any number of current and potential competitors—including premium

5 See, for example, Breaking the box. (2011, April 20). *The Economist*; Can David Fincher save Netflix? (2012, October 4). *Forbes*; Streaming on screens near you. (2016, August 20). *The Economist*.

6 See, for example, The Netflix revolution. (2016, December 10). *The Spectator*; In praise of Netflix. (2017, August 7). *The Spectator*; Streaming could kill UK independent film industry, experts say. (2019, July 7). *The Guardian*; Who should pay for the BBC? (2022, August 22). *The Economist*.

7 See, for example, Netflix conquered the U.S.; the world won't be so easy. (2016, April 4). *Bloomberg*; Inside the binge factory. (2018, June 11). *New York Magazine*.

8 Can Reed Hastings preserve Netflix's culture of innovation as it grows? (2020, September 12). *The Economist*.

> cable channels like HBO (owned by Time Warner, parent of Fortune's publisher) and some of the biggest companies in the tech world—swoop in and deliver a lethal blow, Hastings is now retooling Netflix as a streaming-video company, disrupting his own business before it gets disrupted.[9]

In the age of financialization, especially in the case of media or "new economy" start-ups, such starification of CEOs is usual. For the purposes of communication, on which many of these companies rely for raising funds, "corporation management must accredit the idea that 'somebody's in charge', a 'true leader' and, if possible, someone with qualities which are unlikely to be found in a single person, namely visionary ability as well as budgetary rigour" (Bouquillion, 2008, p. 48). Rapidly, the press took interest in presenting the qualities of some of Netflix's division managers, such as Ted Sarandos, the company's "entertainment savant,"[10] assuming the responsibilities of co-CEO and chief contents manager.

This can be explained by the fact that Netflix's capacity for "disruption" has, since the early 2010s, been presented as its ability to purchase exclusive content based on recommendation algorithms that reduce the risk of misses. Whether in the general or the trade press, analyses have generally explained Netflix's success by relating these two poles: content and algorithms. On the one hand is the quality of its exclusive content, acquired by securing deals with producers and broadcasters or commissioned (and even produced) by the company itself. The content quality is generally celebrated in figures: alongside the acclamation for the choice of actors, the brilliant work of its director, or its multiple Emmy nominations, the series *House of Cards*—which really marked the entry of Netflix into original content—is always presented with a reminder of its "$100m cost for two seasons,"[11] and that "Hollywood is still digesting the numbers."[12] The company's subsequent hit series were also generally advertised with their reported cost, until before long, it was Netflix's overall content spending that was celebrated. A 2013 *Time Magazine* article explains that "an estimated $150 million of the $2.5 billion it is spending this year on acquiring content is going to bankroll Netflix-only programs such as *Orange Is The New Black* and *House of Cards*."[13] From the mid-2010s onward, Netflix's budget for producing and licensing content was to be regularly presented and commented, along with that of competitors in the "streaming wars," as will be shown in the next section. Such big figures

9 Reed Hastings: Leader of the pack. (2010, December 6). *Fortune*.
10 We are still in challenger status. (2020, September 5). *Financial Times*, p. 3.
11 Netflix. (2013, April 23). *Financial Times*, p. 10.
12 Inside Netflix's $100 million house of cards. (2011, April 11). *Hollywood Reporter*.
13 Stream scheme. (2013, November 4). *Time Magazine*.

in content spending are also presented as "big bets"[14] and celebrated for their audacity—an effective way of attracting new subscribers at the expense of more traditional television channels and Pay TV services or film producers.[15]

On the other hand, if Netflix can afford such quality original content and make such bets, it is said to be due to the power of algorithmic recommendation, which should continue to be at the core of the company's strategy for "maintaining the momentum" in the future.[16] As a 2019 article explains, "Netflix has something even brawnier than the combined powers of the X-Men, the Avengers and the Guardians of the Galaxy. It has its algorithm."[17] Big Data analysis is therefore a key element of the "triumph of content" orchestrated under the auspices of Netflix:

> The company has created algorithms to help decide whether to green-light shows (Spacey and Fincher were both popular on the service). Big data even informed the way Netflix promoted *Cards*. Subscribers received different trailers based on their viewing habits: Political junkies saw more of Spacey, while women got more of his wife (Robin Wright). Since then, Netflix has used its data expertise to create and promote other series, such as *Orange Is the New Black*.[18]

Because of its algorithm, Netflix doesn't appear to be constrained by viewer ratings,[19] establishing new ways of producing audiovisual content, allowing directors and producers "more creative freedom,"[20] and targeting "quite precise niches, rather than the broad demographic groups broadcast television depends on"[21] and "extolling the importance of both creative freedom and progressive values."[22] This explains why the company's original series have been "pushing forward more diverse voices than typically seen on broadcast television"—such as transgender representation—an ambition that is presented in comparison as cruelly lacking in traditional broadcasters, who still bear the weight of

14 Netflix targets the bigger picture. (2012, December 6). *Financial Times*.
15 Cutting the cord. (2016, July 16). *The Economist*.
16 4 ways Netflix can maintain the momentum. (2013, October 24). *Fortune*.
17 Disney and chill? (2019, January). *Maclean's*.
18 The triumph of content. (2015, December–2016, January). *Time Magazine*.
19 And the company's shows can't be independently rated. See Netflix says "queen's gambit" draws record 62 million households. (2020, November 23). *Bloomberg*. See also How much longer can Netflix keep ratings a secret? (2013, September 18). *Forbes*.
20 The producer behind "House of Cards" on how Netflix offered creative freedom. (2013, July 18). *Forbes*.
21 Netflix is moving television beyond time-slots and national markets. (2018, June 30). *The Economist*.
22 Netflix's "no rules" culture lands it in PR crisis. (2021, October 23). *Financial Times*, p. 11.

ratings when commissioning a program.[23] In a long article published in 2016, the British novelist and screenwriter Anthony Horowitz wrote:

> Very rarely will a broadcaster in the UK commission as much as ten hours—and certainly not the 50 hours envisaged by Netflix [for its series "*The Crown*"] (the next ten are already in production). You're doing well if you get six. The opening scenes of George VI coughing up blood in the toilet—even the C-word used in a royal limerick—would never have made it on to the BBC or ITV.[24]

As we see, Netflix's "disruption" is presented as strongly relying on its recommendation algorithm. Of course, such comments are fed by the discourse produced by the firm itself, which has always put a lot of emphasis on its new ways of coping with risk. In 2009, it offered $1 million for the best proposition to improve its movie recommendation system's accuracy after a three-year public contest that had seen more than 50,000 people registering for the prize.[25] Since then, the continuous attempts at enhancing its algorithms are discussed in the company's "Technology Blog" where algorithmic models are presented and tested in a self-congratulatory celebration of constant innovation:

> The abundance of source data, measurements and associated experiments allow us to operate a data-driven organization. Netflix has embedded this approach into its culture since the company was founded, and we have come to call it Consumer (Data) Science. Broadly speaking, the main goal of our Consumer Science approach is to innovate for members effectively. The only real failure is the failure to innovate.[26]

The company even sought to increase its reputation by inviting itself into scientific discussion, especially in the domains of consumer research or computer science. In a 2015 article published in the *ACM Transaction on Management Information Systems*, Carlos A. Gomez-Uribe (Netflix's Vice President of Product Innovation) and Neil Hunt (Netflix's Chief Product Officer) both rehearse the narrative of the company's articulation of Big Data analysis and quality or niche content:

> Our recommender system helps us win moments of truth: when a member starts a session and we help that member find something engaging within

23 Netflix's marvelous "the queen's gambit" is the kind of prestige drama TV doesn't make anymore. (2020, October 21). *Time*.

24 The Netflix revolution. (2016, December 10). *The Spectator*.

25 Netflix prize: Another million at stake. (2009, September 22). *Business Week*.

26 Netflix recommendations: Beyond the 5 stars (part 2). (2012, June 20). *Netflix Technology Blog*. https://netflixtechblog.com/netflix-recommendations-beyond-the-5-stars-part-2-d9b96aa399f5

> a few seconds, preventing abandonment of our service for an alternative entertainment option. Personalization enables us to find an audience even for relatively niche videos that would not make sense for broadcast TV models because their audiences would be too small to support significant advertising revenue, or to occupy a broadcast or cable channel time slot.
> (Gomez-Uribe & Hunt, 2015, p. 13:6)

All throughout the past decade, Netflix's CEO rarely missed an opportunity to highlight the claims of its algorithmic recommendation system, summarized in a speech given in 2016 at a Las Vegas consumer electronics show: "One day we hope to get so good at suggestions that we're able to show you exactly the right film or TV show for your mood when you turn on Netflix."[27] Such discourses have since been widely developed by tech and media analysis firms regularly quoted in the trade press, such as MoffetNathanson for whom "competition is not limited to who has the best content; it is also framed around who has the best tech,"[28] or by financial information companies like S&P Global, which includes recommendation and algorithms in its analysis of Netflix's strategies.[29] It is therefore no wonder that the theme of algorithms heralding a new era of media capitalism has even started to seep into debates in cultural economics (Hadida et al., 2021; Aguiar & Waldfogel, 2018).

## . . . to More Traditional Structuration

It is enlightening to relate these "disruption" discourses to Netflix's trajectory, particularly since its entry into content production, starting with investment in the Norwegian series *Lillehammer* in 2012 and especially with *House of Cards* in 2013. While algorithms are supposed to transform the ways in which programs are presented to viewers and, in turn, to direct specific content spending, it seems that, on the contrary, the company's strategy tends to comply with the traditional logic of the audiovisual industries.

As we argued in the previous section, since the mid-2010s, the company's total content spending has been regularly publicized and relayed in the press. This amount has grown exponentially (Figure 4.1), along with its share of original production. Consequently, Netflix's produced content assets have grown significantly, even exceeding its licensed assets in 2021 (Figure 4.2).

27 Quoted in How to devise the perfect recommendation algorithm. (2017, February 9). *The Economist*.

28 Quoted in How Hollywood's biggest stars are losing their clout. (2011, November 8). *The Economist*.

29 Analysts question Netflix strategy as costs and competition grow. (2019, August 15). *S&P Global—Market Intelligence*. www.spglobal.com/marketintelligence/en/news-insights/latest-news-headlines/analysts-question-netflix-strategy-as-costs-and-competition-grow-53498213

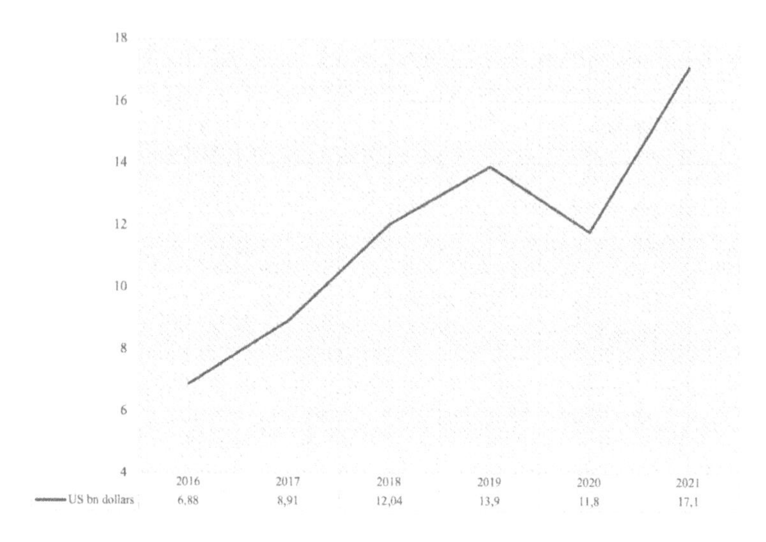


*Figure 4.1* Netflix's content spending (worldwide, in billion US dollars).

Source: Statista; Netflix

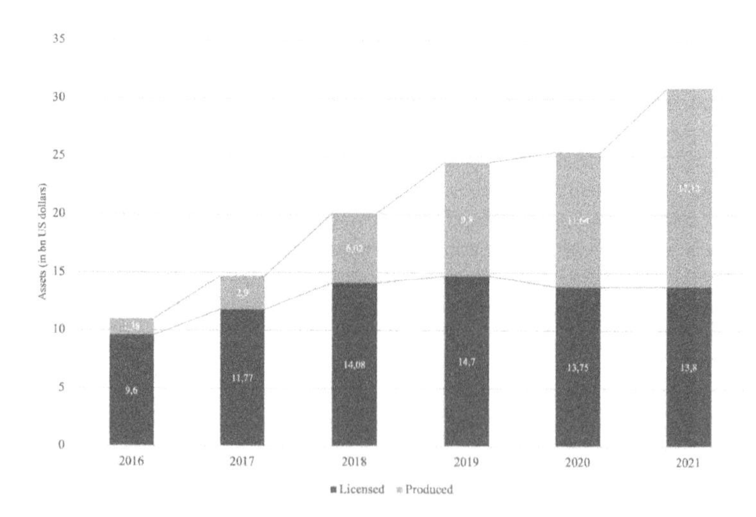


*Figure 4.2* Netflix's content assets, by type (worldwide, in billion US dollars).

It is therefore obvious that the company has clearly put the ownership of a large catalog of premium content at the center of its strategy since the past decade. In particular, the production of original programs has been a fundamental element since the establishment of competing SVOD services, including that of Disney, which stopped licensing its own content to Netflix in 2018 in favor of its own platform (a project under consideration since 2015).[30]

Interestingly, here again, this "strike-back"[31] from Disney, which "in its 97th year has decided [that] its television future lies in streaming"[32] has been widely commented as the comeback of the "empire," and its traditional strategy based on content production and continued investment in blockbusters,[33] as opposed to Netflix's strategy based on recommendation. In this clash of giants, the figure of Bob Iger is mythologized as the man who, upon taking over as Disney's CEO in 2005,

> felt sure that, in an era of proliferating content, big brands would become more valuable—the bigger the better. The company went on to spend $15.5bn to amass an arsenal of content brands that became the envy of the media world: Pixar Animation Studios, Marvel Entertainment and, in 2012, Lucasfilm, maker of "Star Wars."[34]

But is Netflix's strategy finally very different? Most of the rivalry seems to lie in content spending figures, securing licensed assets and reinforcing original production. As Perticoz (2019, §14) notes, it seems that Netflix's and Disney's trajectories turn out to be rather convergent.

> More specifically, since 2015, it appears that Disney and Netflix have each been trying to fill what they have identified as their own respective shortcomings in order to position themselves as the "paying audiovisual media of the 21th century," thus competing directly with Pay TV offers.

Incidentally, this competition over Pay TV offers is also worth analyzing in terms of Netflix's strategy. The numerous comparisons between the SVOD service and traditional networks like HBO regularly note that "Netflix is paying far more than the prestige channel ever did,"[35] or for that matter, national broadcasters. The comparison holds because, in its rise to becoming a global

30 Disney's new platform could become the streaming king for kids. (2017, August 9). *Forbes*.
31 Disney/streaming: The empire strikes back. (2020, December 12). *Financial Times*, p. 18.
32 Disney Plus streams ahead of legacy assets. (2020, December 7). *Financial Times*, p. 7.
33 Mass entertainment in the digital age is still about blockbusters, not endless choice. (2017, February 9). *The Economist*.
34 Ibid.
35 Netflix zombies. (2017, June 29). *Forbes*, p. 99.

content provider, Netflix has commissioned content from many local producers from the mid-2010s onward. In Europe, for example, the company became the largest single commissioner of new European scripted TV content in 2020, in front of ZDF (Germany), the BBC and FranceTV (three public broadcasters).[36]

This "all-out" spending is often lauded as a strategy of "diversity," enabled by the company's recommendation algorithms. But, in reality, it resembles a very traditional catalogue strategy of " 'throwing mud . . . against the wall' to see what sticks" (Hesmondhalgh, 2013, p. 22). As *The Economist* notes in a 2016 article on Netflix, "In the next year there will be new television series in Italian, German, Spanish and Japanese, and the second series of a French political drama, 'Marseille', starring Gérard Depardieu. Some of these shows will be excellent, and some will not."[37] And in fact, some were successes, and most were not, as is traditionally the rule in the culture industry. Of course, this "diversity" strategy is sometimes imposed by regulatory measures, notably in Asia.[38] In general, however, Netflix is building a worldwide catalogue of titles of which only a small proportion will be successful, offsetting a majority of misses. Often, this strategy is accompanied by the use of star actors or creators, locally as well as internationally (Martin Scorsese and Shonda Rhimes are regularly cited).[39] Incidentally, even local successes, such as the Korean series *Squid Game*, eventually became global hits,[40] encouraged by the global strategy of the platform, which also in turn adapts some global hits to local markets[41]—once again, a traditional strategy of audience maximization.

For the most part, much of this expenditure is financed by long-term debt (which has caused a few minor panics in financial markets in the wake of stock market slides). In what is ultimately a prolongation of structural changes in the media since the 1980s, extensively documented by political economy theorists (McChesney, 2015; Hardy, 2014; Bouquillion, 2008), Netflix is forced to rely on continual exponential growth in order to retain the favorable valuations of the financial sector which, in turn, provides it with the funds necessary for worldwide investments in a traditional strategy of mass production and cost spreading. In this regard, recommendation algorithms, praised for their ability to reduce the risks of investment in content, do not appear to really transform the economy of audiovisual production, while the high costs of content spending always elevate the barriers to entry even more.

36 Source: Ampere Analysis. See Video-on-demand—market data analysis & forecast. (2022, June). *Statista*.

37 Streaming on screens near you. (2016, August 20). *The Economist*.

38 Netflix plans to double spending on original content in Asia. (2020, December 1). *Bloomberg*.

39 Netflix is moving television beyond time-slots and national markets. (2018, June 30). *The Economist*.

40 Squid game takes Korean soft power up a notch. (2021, October 7). *Bloomberg*.

41 Netflix plans $500 million spending in Korea to crack Asia. (2021, February 25). *Bloomberg*.

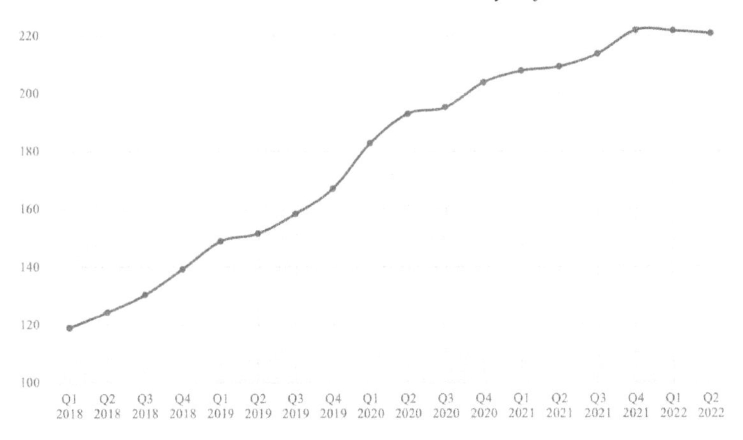


*Figure 4.3* Netflix's paid subscribers (worldwide, in millions).

Source: Statista; Netflix

Furthermore, when a crisis hit the company in the spring of 2022, with a worldwide loss of subscribers after a tangible slowdown in 2021 (Figure 4.3), Netflix's CEO revealed that the platform was exploring the possibility of launching ad-supported subscriptions.[42] If this possibility comes to pass, Netflix will move closer to the traditional logic of commercial television and its newer variants intensively introduced by digital media (Fuchs, 2014), and centered on the extensive production of precise user data. In fact, this is where its technical system could be most effective, centered on the collection of user's watching habits.

## "Especially for You": A Mythology of Algorithms in the Transformation of Media Capitalism

The question remains, however, of the real place of algorithms in the audiovisual industries: does this mean that the emphasis on algorithms is mere propaganda, disseminated to the media (and even to universities) in order to sell SVOD subscriptions and to keep share prices high? Such assumptions could easily be made but would probably miss what is at stake in contemporary transformations of capitalist strategies in the media.

As has been well documented (see e.g., Mattelart, 2003), the deployment of media and communication technologies is always accompanied by discourses of legitimation, which are generally concentrated in a syntagm or

42 Netflix plans to launch cheaper ad-supported plans. (2022, April 19). *The Hollywood Reporter*.

formula. These, which have proliferated greatly since the end of the Second World War, open up vast promises—always aborted and renewed—of social transformation. Such discourses circulate with their share of enthusiastic proponents and horrified critics, be they in the industry (that knows how to use these discourses to sell products), in civil society, in politics, in the media and in academia and can therefore have effects in the real world. But, as Vincent Mosco explains in *The Digital Sublime*—focusing on the discourses around *cyberspace*—these narratives should not be treated as mere (dis)information but rather as *myths* that "mean more than falsehoods or cons" (Mosco, 2004, p. 3). Thus, their analysis "involves more than proving [them] to be false. It means figuring out why the myth exists, why it is so important to people, what it means, and what it tells us about people's hopes and dreams" (ibid., p. 29). Indeed, taken as *myths*, the various syntagms accompanying the deployment of the communication technologies are to be considered as a speech for which "truth is no guarantee" (Barthes, 1972, p. 122). Therefore, limiting theoretical work to taking part in a debate "for or against," "enthusiastic or dubious," only reinforces the narrative. This is why myths are also largely fed by journalistic debates: "while journalistic rapture is certainly important to advancing the cause, it is the cautionary tale that adds depth to the vision" (Mosco, 2004, p. 44).

There is no question here of sweeping aside or underestimating the legitimate concerns that the algorithmic systems of recommendation raise about privacy. But if we are, then, to consider the discourses on algorithms and their place in the future of media as *myths*, the question is not whether the predictions are good, or encourage diversity, or whether, if they improve, they will one day be the only element of decision in cultural production or distribution, resulting in a limitation of consumers' media horizons. Indeed, both dimensions are present in the narrative and, although we have until now focused on positive commentaries, it must be noted how much the possibility of recommendation algorithms that actually *work* is at the heart of many negative reactions. For example, in a very subtle opinion article in 2019, the British columnist and writer Sarah Ditum warns that Netflix's system "has the potential to create a closed world where everything you encounter resembles something you already like."[43] Similar warnings have been issued by academic authors (see Alexander, 2016).

But what do these discourses mean and what is their place in the history of capitalism in the media? Taking them together reveals the extent to which narratives surrounding recommendation algorithms are in line with the historical analysis of the culture industry by Max Horkheimer and Theodor Adorno (2002). The products of mass culture have a common characteristic: they all resemble one another. But this characteristic makes them contradict the very

43 Digital dispatches. (2019, April 5–11). *The New Statesman*, p. 29.

concept of culture, as well as the liberal imaginary on which the very force of the culture industry is based. The culture industry is thus also characterized by the controlled production of differentiation ("pseudo-individualization" in the words of Adorno, 1941) until "something is provided for everyone so that no one can escape; differences are hammered home and propagated" (Horkheimer & Adorno, 2002, p. 97). In fact, the whole history of the media is marked by this tension between content standardization and a hint of novelty, which camouflages it. With their "user generated content," online media platforms like YouTube have been deployed within a "collaborative" imaginary and a rhetoric of "participation," in an attempt to address this tension by putting consumers back at the center of cultural production (Fuchs, 2014), as if standardization could be overcome by users being their own content producers. The myth of recommendation algorithms deploys a rhetoric of the same nature that takes reception into account as well as production. It promises plethoric catalogs of content, thus flattering the appetite for culture and, at the same time, pretending that the industry has produced something special for everyone, for each one to find and enjoy.

Analyzing a minor hit song of 1940 recorded by Bonnie Baker the year before, Adorno shows how its very title—"Especially for You"—concentrates the whole problematic of the culture industry:

> The sheer idiocy of a mass product created especially for you assumes the character of a ghastly necessity. Individual needs have been so ruthlessly eliminated from the product that they have to be invoked like magic formulae to prevent the customer from becoming aware of the murderous ritual of which he is the victim.
>
> (Adorno, 2000, p. 44)

Behind the veneer of digital ultra-modernity, the myth of algorithmic recommendation as directing cultural production and distribution is a continuation of this magical invocation. Accepting the standardization of cultural content and the consequent standardization of viewer behavior, it provides a chimeric remedy, namely that in this standardization, each person will have the right to his or her share of what has been produced "especially" for his or her market segment.

## References

Adorno, T. W. (1941). On popular music. *Zeitschrift Für Sozialforschung*, *9*(1), 17–48.

Adorno, T. W. (2000). *Quasi una fantasia: Essays on modern music*. Verso.

Aguiar, L., & Waldfogel, J. (2018). Netflix: Global hegemon or facilitator of frictionless digital trade? *Journal of Cultural Economics*, *42*(3), 419–445. https://doi.org/10.1007/s10824-017-9315-z

Alexander, N. (2016). Catered to your future self: Netflix's "predictive personalization" and the mathematization of taste. In K. McDonald & D. Smith-Roswey (Eds.),

*The Netflix effect: Technology and entertainment in the 21st century* (pp. 81–97). Bloomsbury.
Balio, T. (1976). *United artists: The company built by the stars*. University of Wisconsin Press.
Barthes, R. (1972). *Mythologies*. Hill and Wang.
Bouquillion, P. (2008). *Les industries de la culture et de la communication: Les stratégies du capitalisme*. PUG.
Chapman, J. (2003). *Cinemas of the world*. Reaktion Books.
Finn, E. (2017). *What Algorithms Want: Imagination in the Age of Computing*, MIT Press.
Flichy, P. (1980). *Les industries de l'imaginaire: Pour une analyse économique des médias*. PUG.
Fuchs, C. (2014). *Digital labour and Karl Marx*. Routledge.
Garnham, N. (1990). *Capitalism and communication*. Sage.
Gomez-Uribe, C. A., & Hunt, N. (2015). The Netflix recommender system: Algorithms, business value, and innovation. *ACM Transactions on Management Information Systems*, *6*(4), 13:1–13:19.
Hadida, A. L., Lampel, J., Walls, W. D., & Joshi, A. (2021). Hollywood studio filmmaking in the age of Netflix: A tale of two institutional logics. *Journal of Cultural Economics*, *45*(2), 213–238. https://doi.org/10.1007/s10824-020-09379-z
Hardy, J. (2014). *Critical political economy of the media: An introduction*. Routledge.
Hesmondhalgh, D. (2013). *The cultural industries*. Sage.
Horkheimer, M., & Adorno, T. W. (2002). *Dialectic of enlightenment*. Stanford University Press.
Lacroix, J.-G., & Tremblay, G. (1997). The "information society" and the cultural industries theory. *Current Sociology*, *45*(4), 1–154.
Mattelart, A. (2003). *The information society: An introduction*. Sage.
McChesney, R. W. (2015). *Rich media, poor democracy: Communication politics in dubious times*. The New Press.
Meehan, E. R. (1984). Ratings and the institutional approach: A third answer to the commodity question. *Critical Studies in Mass Communication*, 216–225.
Mœglin, P. (2007). *Changing socioeconomic models*. Omic.
Mosco, V. (2004). *The digital sublime: Myth, power, and cyberspace*. MIT Press.
Perticoz, L. (2019). Filière de l'audiovisuel et plateformes SVOD: Une analyse croisée des stratégies de Disney et Netflix. *Tic&Société*, *13*(1–2), 323–353. https://doi.org/10.4000/ticetsociete.3470
Prindle, D. F. (1993). *Risky business*. Westview Press.
Schatz, T. (1981). *Hollywood genres: Formulas, filmmaking and the studio system*. Random House.
Smythe, D. W. (1977). Communications: Blindspot of Western Marxism. *Canadian Journal of Political and Social Theory*, *1*(3), 1–21.
Tryon, C. (2015). TV Got Better: Netflix's Original Programming Strategies and Binge Viewing. *Media Industries*, *2*(2), 104–116.
Uricchio, W. (2017). Data, Culture and the Ambivalence of Algorithms. In K. Van Es & M. T. Schäfer (eds.), *The Datafied Society* (pp. 125–38). Amsterdam University Press.
Wasko, J. (2005). Critiquing Hollywood: The political economy of motion pictures. In C. C. Moul (Ed.), *A concise handbook of movie industry economics* (pp. 5–31). Cambridge University Press.
Williams, R. (1974). *Television: Technology and cultural form*. Routledge.

# 5 Counter-hegemonic AI

## The Role of Artisanal Identity in the Design of Automation for a Liberated Economy

*Matthew Garvin, Ron Eglash, Kwame Porter Robinson, Lionel Robert, Mark Guzdial and Audrey Bennett*

### Introduction

In discussions of AI and social justice, work on bias is often forefronted to the exclusion of all else. The emphasis is not unwarranted: examples of bias in AI and related data-dependent systems can be found in health disparities (Veinot et al., 2018); in trans, intersex and nonbinary populations (Cirillo et al., 2020); medical genetics (Nature Editorial Board, 2020; Pennisi, 2021); and decision-making across both state and civic spheres (Kapur, 2021). We emphasize these examples to be clear that we are not saying that working to expose and eliminate such bias is irrelevant. It is indeed a necessary component, but alone it is not sufficient. Making exploitation the same for everyone in a hegemonic system does not change the system's fundamental harms. As Costanza-Chock (2020, p. 72) puts it: "Employment diversity is a necessary first move, but it is not the horizon of collective liberation and ecological sustainability."

As Marx pointed out long ago, mass production workers have value "alienated" from them in multiple senses of the word. Firstly, most of the value they create is taken away with little return. Secondly, the object they create becomes less meaningful to them if it is an assembly line of widgets. And thirdly, the workplace itself makes them feel more like a cog in the machine. Capital is the accumulation of this alienated value, and Marx saw technology as a kind of further condensation that would disempower workers. Prior to computers, this was somewhat mitigated by a reinstatement effect: workers were displaced but technology created new tasks, such as repair, monitoring, the rise of skilled specialists and so on, which reinstated labor. But Acemoglu and Restrepo (2019) provide an economic analysis indicating that this is not the case for computational technologies: there have been "stronger displacement effects and considerably weaker reinstatement effects during the last 30 years than the decades before" (p. 6). What we might call hyper-extraction—capital turning labor into alienated value, computing turning

DOI: 10.4324/9781003299875-5

capital into technologies of alienation—makes it likely that we will see a future of enhanced forms of deskilling, monotony and precarity (Fuchs, 2014; Lindley et al., 2019; McRobbie, 2018).

That's not to say this is predetermined or inevitable. Acemoglu and Restrepo also point out the influence of economic policy: for example, capital investments in technology are incentivized by tax breaks, while payroll taxes encourage less hiring. Even more influential, stock prices rise and fall based on how "visionary" a company rhetoric presents itself, and while that may be temporary, the advantages can be locked in. Tesla's claim to be seeking a fully automated factory earned far more from such attention-seeking and rhetoric effects than any cost savings gained by shedding workers (Acemoglu & Restrepo, 2019). In sum, automation of this type—high displacement and low reinstatement—is not an inevitable aspect of technological evolution but rather a self-fulfilling prophecy.

The end result of this process is not necessarily joblessness but rather lower pay and more subservient jobs such as the service sector and gig economy. A dramatic decline in labor share—the percentage of profits going to pay worker salaries (blue and white collar alike)—is thus a development directly linked to automation (Acemoglu & Restrepo, 2020; Grossman & Oberfield, 2021). With so much technological momentum (Hughes, 1994), altering this trajectory will require systemic change, upending wealth inequality and its stratification by geography, identity and other social markers. Yet the best-known alternative—the socialist replacement of capitalism with state ownership—has, at least in the majority of historical cases, been marked by very similar kinds of wealth inequality and environmental harm (Eglash, 2016, 2018; Mazurski, 1991). For that reason (and others), the field of design is increasingly a site for the search for alternative futures. With AI poised to make such transformative impacts, its redesign as an agent of positive change is frequently mentioned in speculative design, design fiction and other visionary processes (Jang & Nam, 2022; Manton & Aga, 2021; Simeone et al., 2022). Can technological systems—even the technology itself—be redesigned for less extractive, less alienated, more liberated kinds of work in both capitalist and socialist economies?

We have focused on artisans, defined broadly as anyone doing work that is unalienated (more about that shortly), in part because they are well positioned to go beyond thinking of design participants as merely a compendium of local needs and assets and engage them as actors in longer histories of resistance to colonialism, racism, sexism, classism and other forms of domination. While that methodology could in theory be carried out with any community, there are unique aspects in the ways that a counter-hegemonic identity has thrived as both political awareness and lifeways of physical practice among artisans.

If we think about varieties of artisanal practice—Native American crafters, urban farmers, Black braiding shops, automobile customizers, repair shops, and other small-scale localized crafting in food, furniture, textiles, adornment, education, entertainment and so on—one can immediately see the import. They can bridge racialized gaps that few others can traverse; they represent heritage practices that colonialism failed to extinguish, and they tap into long histories of unalienated value production that has held out against both communist and capitalist domination (Sirois, 2020). The US Small Business Administration does not count artisanal as a category, but they do track a reasonable proxy: single worker-owned or "nonemployer" business. "Compared to employer owners, owners of nonemployer businesses are younger and more diverse in terms of race, ethnicity, and gender. About one-third of nonemployer businesses are owned by minorities and four in ten are owned by women" (SBA Profiles, 2018).

Our position is that if we are to support more equitable futures of work *with* AI, it will be important to draw on artisans as collaborators and as bearers of knowledge (Munck, 2019) that can illuminate some of the strategies key to the survival of unalienated labor amidst technosocial change. While our main focus in this chapter is on the generic category of artisan in struggles against domination, elsewhere we have mapped out similar descriptions with a decolonial focus on Black, Native and Latinx communities (Eglash et al., 2021; Eglash & Foster, 2017).

## Artisans in the History of Political Economy

Artisans vary in their sociopolitical status from one culture to the next. For example, blacksmiths in traditional African societies were typically seen as holding special spiritual power, while the artisanal peasantry of ancient China typically held a very low status (Ehmer, 2001). Marx described European artisans in two different historical moments: the early era of guilds and later era of manufacture. In the guild era he saw the more pristine notion of *kleine Warenproduktion* (small commodity production), in which he maintained one could find vestiges of pre-capitalist, unalienated forms of labor (Ehmer, 2001). But that began to change in the era of manufacture. For example in 1814 England repealed the laws requiring apprenticeship; as a result there were artisan protests as companies began to hire untrained workers in an early attempt to organize what we now refer to as "sweatshop" labor (Rule, 1987). On the other hand, in Germany artisans became more synonymous with what Marx and others disparagingly referred to as the "labor aristocracy" (Hanagan, 1977; Hobsbawm, 1984)—apprenticed journeymen whose skills were in high demand. From Marx's view, these were barriers to the revolution. There is still a lively debate about these well-paid artisans among scholars today. Post (2010, p. 3) maintains that both historically and today, "relatively well-paid workers have and continue to play a leading rôle in radical and revolutionary working-class organizations and struggles." Cope (2013) rejects this portrait, maintaining that because of colonial and neocolonial transfer of wealth, skilled workers in the global north have been enabling capital's domination globally in the ways Marx first proposed.

In contrast to Marx, anarchists such as Kropotkin saw these highly skilled artisans as much more fundamental, the opposite of a barrier. In the Jura hills of Switzerland, Kropotkin spent time with the little towns and villages engaged in different aspects of watchmaking. He observed that their intellectual development and expressive autonomy resulted from the decentralized organization of the watch trade and the more egalitarian relations that manifest through such labor arrangements, and saw in this a model for a more egalitarian future (Eglash, 2018; Kropotkin, 1899; Oved, 1992). Vuilleumier (2018) cautions against reducing the watchmakers themselves to labels like anarchist, as there were diversities of views. But that was Kropotkin's point: their autonomous political development was freely self-determined, and in the end they did oppose Marx's attempt to turn the International Workingmen's Association into a centralized authority.

Thus for Marx, skilled artisans were an example of the labor that everyone could enjoy in the future, but only if we first relinquished all rights to a centralized communist authority. For Kropotkin, that aspect of autonomy *was* the revolution, and it could be broadened to the general populace by democratizing the economy, not centralizing it. This distinction is sometimes understood as Marx's Machiavellian approach—the ends justify the means—versus Kropotkin's more Gandhian approach, that the means need to reflect the end goal. Kropotkin was not consistent on all fronts, but when it came to artisans, the comparison holds (Cleaver, 1994).

Links between artisanal labor and these radical visions of liberation were also promoted by Kropotkin's friend, the artist and designer William Morris, and can be found throughout artisanal labor history, from Morris' era of the arts and crafts movement, to today's maker movements and craftivism protests (Krugh, 2014). Our work on artisanal identity and counter-hegemonic AI is thus aligned with this idea of the transformative potential in creative independent labor. Artisanal identity is particularly important in that it offers an example of making ends and means convergent in the tradition of what is often termed "prefigurative politics" (Leach, 2013). One hallmark of authoritarian movements is that of ends and means contradictions: violence today with the promise of a future end to violence; loyal obedience with the promise of future democracy. In contrast, artisans (at least those who are sincere) seek a future of dignified, meaningful work by carrying that out in the present day; they "prefigure" a future that is, if political transformation follows their lead, attainable by all.

## Artisan Identity and the Counter-hegemonic Entrepreneur

To some extent, the goals and motivations of the artisan and the entrepreneur can be viewed as opposites. In the Western sense, entrepreneurs are typically characterized by their calculated risk-taking and aggressive pursuit of growth and return on investment (Baumol, 1993; Gartner, 1990; Knight, 1921).

Typically profit considerations vastly outweigh any interest in the particulars of a product or process.

The positive feedback loop of capitalism as "money in pursuit of more of itself" has been strongly implicated in global environmental destruction, the rising tide of authoritarian attacks on democracy, rising inequality, and other social and ecological disasters (Sosteric, 2018). By putting quality, humanistic style, sustainability and meaningful work ahead of profits, artisanal approaches to entrepreneurship (and related forms such as "triple bottom line" [Elkington, 2018]) may be the only sustainable way to conduct capitalism in the long run. But this begs the question: How do artisans survive financially if not focused on profits? How can they compete against ruthless profit-centered competitors? And if not expanding as big as possible, what are the goals, business practices and economic strategies?

Because historically, artisan entrepreneurs typically sold their items in small shops or artisan fairs (Greiner, 1998), one of the most significant constraints about growing an artisanal enterprise has been attracting more customers. Scaling this kind of operation requires either more storefronts or attending more fairs. Both options, in turn, require more dedication to administrative duties and less to craft. Generally speaking, now that the internet has become more pervasive, artisan entrepreneurs have reduced such impediments, and their goods are more accessible to a broader pool of customers (Kuhn & Galloway, 2015; Luckman, 2015). In addition, there has been a complementary shift in consumer-based social movements, such as sustainability, farm to table and "buy local," making artisan products more appealing (Carroll & Wheaton, 2009). In fact, Luckman (2018) reported that one of the biggest challenges artisan entrepreneurs seem to be facing is how to manage this explosive growth in consumer demand while not getting too big.

Solomon and Mathias (2020) conducted 34 interviews across a wide variety of artisan entrepreneurs and concluded that there are two aspects of identity at work. First is a strong sense of oppositional identity, "who we are not," for example, corporate-owned mass producers. On the flip side they describe the relational identity, "who we are," that is, the notion of artisanal authenticity (which will be critical to our later discussion of AI). They found oppositional identity expressed in four ways:

1. Craft over mass production
2. Independence over conglomeration
3. Community/localism over distant corporatism
4. A nonfinancial focus over profit maximization

The Butchers Guild (n.d.) exemplifies the first principle in their mission statement, "We need better practices and better meat. And as a society, we need to eat less of it." Of course, any association's public mission statement would emphasize a commitment to maintaining a quality product. But asking people to eat less meat offers such a striking contrast to the goals and values of meat processors and ranchers with a capitalist growth mentality.

The second principle, prioritizing independence over conglomeration, again requires some sacrifice; for example it causes some artisan entrepreneurs to turn down capital from investors seeking to maintain a silent partnership. The third, commitments with the local community, allows them to connect with residents and potential customers in ways corporations cannot. Not only does The Butchers Guild advance strong opposition to their corporate counterparts, but they indict them for ruining the food system as a whole:

> The Butchers Guild stands in the guild tradition of maintaining a moral code within a trade. Butchers in the United States have lost their cohesion and support network as the food system has become dangerously centralized, and the centralization killed the demand for skilled artisans. We see the future of food based in localized food communities that require the knowledge of the butcher, and we are fostering this generation of craftsmen.
>
> (The Butchers Guild, n.d.)

A final characteristic of the oppositional identity is the nonfinancial focus. As we will detail next, artisan entrepreneurs tend to place concerns about authenticity in their craft over any strategic growth model. However, by de-emphasizing growth, Solomon and Mathias (2020) argue they create the kinds of authenticity and product quality that encourages expansion. This is sometimes channeled into advancing a larger movement, including educating and supplying a growing consumer base, creating demand for suppliers who themselves have made commitments to sustainable localism, or providing better support for their employees with above-average pay and benefits. Of course, such claims may simply be attempts to rationalize decisions made out of self-interest while maintaining a positive reputation. But Solomon and Mathias (2020) found that follow-up interviews with members of the community seem to support professed desires to strengthen the social fabric.

To summarize, the counter-hegemonic identity of the artisan entrepreneur manifests itself in a somewhat paradoxical manner, surviving as a for-profit entity while eschewing a profit-centric perspective. The goal of artisanal enterprise appears to be unalienated production that allows economic survival while simultaneously circulating value, rather than simply extracting it, thus nurturing its unalienated generation in the outlying infrastructure (skills, workers, supply chains and so on) and within the communities in which they are embedded. We hypothesize that advances in digital technologies, properly designed and politically deployed, could be used to leverage this worthy set of goals into practices broadly adopted across the entire economy. That is, if the means of innovation were developed at the grassroots, such that the artisans themselves guided AI and related developments.

## Artisans in the History of Automation

Jura region watchmakers of the 19th century again provide an interesting example. Their approach was reminiscent of the Italian "flexible specialization" described by Piore and Sabel (1984) in which small firms specialized in components that were assembled into more complex products, achieving lower prices, higher quality and yet maintaining autonomy. Landes (1984) describes how the Jura artisans carried this out by selectively adopting home-production innovation. In many other cases, the trend has been one in which innovation undermined autonomy (Hanagan, 1977). Nevertheless, this was a gradual and uneven process, and often the counter-hegemonic identity of artisans survived. We will examine this in three domains: the adoption of technology when faced with job displacement; the maintenance of production independence in the face of industrial appropriation; and the maintenance of race, class and gender diversity when faced with gentrification.

While employers specialized their products, artisans generalized their skill sets (Hanagan, 1977). Apprentices moved from shop to shop and adapted their talents to a wide range of different work contexts. Successive rounds of mechanization and the shifting division of labor did not erode all of their skills, and in some cases prompted innovation, as in the Swiss case. Hanagan (1977) summarizes the process as assimilation: "the machine ate away at his technical mastery one bit at a time, and, gradually, the artisanal worker faded into the skilled industrial worker." That is surely true in some cases. Noble (1978) for example detailed a much more abrupt transition for machinists whose jobs were undermined by numerically controlled machine tools, now called computer aided manufacturer (CAM) in the 1950s. But focusing on machinists provides only a very narrow window on artisanal labor: one focused on male-dominated or masculinized work that excludes industries such as textiles, food, adornment, entertainment, home life, exercise, education and other sectors where artisanal niches have flourished, and that are generally more race and gender diverse.

The contemporary discourse surrounding automation in postindustrial society notes the continuation of artisanal survival; indeed creative industries are often described as relatively safe compared to the low-paid, repetitive labor of factory work, hospitality and agriculture (Eglash et al., 2020; Friedman, 2010; Katz, 2014; McMeel, 2021). This has led to increasing interest in what is being described as artisan entrepreneurship. Drawing on Tregear (2005), Pret and Cogan (2019) define artisan entrepreneurs as "individuals who produce and sell products or services which possess a distinct artistic value resulting from a high degree of manual input." The "manual" part of this definition creates an unnecessary opposition between artisanal identity and automation. Far better is Katz's (2014) "personal flair at each stage of the job," which leaves open diverse possibilities for human-machine interaction, collaboration and allocation.

We can make a further distinction, which is the contrast between industrial appropriation of artisanal labor and its opposite of independent artisanal entrepreneurship. Industrial appropriation under communism is carried out through the fiction of legal ownership through the state: if this is "the people's factory" then you are a "counter-revolutionary" if you protest in cases where it is exploitative and underpaid (Burawoy, 1990). Industrial appropriation under capitalism is carried out by two methods. The first is simply marketing: for example the three largest snack food companies in the world are Nestle ("Artisan collection baking chips"), PepsiCo (Stubborn brand "craft sodas") and Mondelēz ("Wheat Thins Artisan Cheese Crackers"). The second is the gig economy: by creating dependency on platforms and other kinds of precarious extraction, corporations maintain sufficient illusions of freedom such that they can tap into creative labor and yet have enough control ("algorithmic extraction") that they reap the lion's share of the value (Wood & Lehdonvirta, 2021; Zietlow, 2020). In contrast, artisans who develop an independently sustainable business, belong to a worker collective, or in some other way have direct control over the conditions of production and the fruits of their labor can be understood to engage in independent artisan entrepreneurship.

Finally, we should note the distinction between the race, class and gender diversity of most small-scale artisanal enterprises and the gentrification that has come with increased interest, funding and technology access. We support the use of the term "artisan" to describe designers and makers that use computing technologies, design software and digital fabrication equipment like 3D printers (Kneese et al., 2014). But our focus on counter-hegemonic practices among artisans requires attention to the ways that artisanal identifications can be appropriated to maintain race, class and gender power structures using digital technologies. For example, the artisanal culture in Brooklyn has been described as connecting hipsters to the same neighborhoods they are simultaneously gentrifying (Tanenbaum, 2014; Wasielewski, 2018). Not all artisan entrepreneurs exemplify the characteristics of the counter-hegemonic identity, and here is where Marx's critique of labor aristocracy (Cope, 2013) perhaps gains more validity. While we argue that the figure of the white, middle-class hipster artisan is overemphasized (why not pay equal attention to hyper-modern Black artisans in Brooklyn?[1]) it is crucial to analyze the link between digital skills and race and class boundaries. If "bottom-up" transformation has a digital glass ceiling, it offers no real transformation at all. With that in mind, we examine how digital technology intersects artisanal identity more closely.

1 Not hard to find, for example, there are 30 Black-owned stores in the "design" category at www.blackownedbrooklyn.com, and that is not counting artisans typically excluded from consideration, such as the 83 (by Google search) Black hair salons in Brooklyn, many of which incorporate digital technologies in their application of Black aesthetics to social media's visual and narrative digital technologies, or what Brock (2020) calls "the Black technocultural matrix."

## The Intersection of Digital Technology and Artisanal Identity

Luckman (2015, 2018; Luckman & Andrew, 2020) notes that artisanal activities cover a spectrum between those more focused on conceptual/virtual domains of design and those more focused on physical creation. But the analysis of creative practices shows that even virtual design is carried out as a kind of feedback loop, "a conversation between the designer and the materials of the situation" as Schön (1992) famously put it. This emphasizes the ways in which the design evolves as we try out various configurations and conceptualizations and adapt the design as the human and nonhuman agencies of the situation respond (Pickering, 1995). Thus, the artisan is not necessarily only those who occupy one end of that spectrum. Rather, their work style is better defined as those least inclined to create labor apartheid—abstractions between themselves and those carrying out the work—and that of course is at a maximum for worker-owned business.

That is not merely on principle: Schön's point in his prescient 1992 essay was opposing the kinds of AI development that ignored this fact and created technologies that would destroy an alliance between the ideation and implementation sides. Thus, there is convergence between the ethical principles at stake—less exploitation when workers and owners are one—and the epistemological principles, where head and hand, input and output, risks and responsibilities are working in reciprocal synthesis. Thus, there is some inherent prevention of value alienation tied to the styles of work and creative assets of artisans, even in the case of digital tools.

Sennett's (2008, 2020) decades of research on craft, including that involving 3D printing and similar technologies, makes a strong case that the connection between head and hand does indeed survive the introduction of more sophisticated tools, including those of the digital era:

> We worked for a couple of years at Harvard Medical School to try to find out why hand drawing can be more innovative than CAD design. Their argument was that the sheer difficulty of drawing by hand, the uncertainty of how the hand will move, serves as a stimulus to innovation. Resistance and difficulty produce skill. The architectural designer needs both CAD and the pencil—the pencil to think, CAD to execute. . . . Rather than craftsmanship, particularly hand-craftsmanship, being put out of date by any kind of mechanical labor, we have to have a more sophisticated notion of connecting the bodily work we do to the mental labor we do.
>
> (34–35)

By making this broader definition, we open the possibility of including independent software developers. The purely virtual area of work is not disqualifying, as long as they meet the other criteria. Most crucially, Katz's notion of "personal flair" would eliminate as artisans the kinds of low-paid "making code to specs" that are often the stereotype of gig workers. But Irani and Silberman (2016) noted that this emphasis on gig workers as an alienated virtual assembly line in the case of Amazon Mechanical Turk is quite unfounded: the Turkers' opposition to low pay should not be conflated with a lack of agency or creativity in their work. Tremblay and Genin (2008) report that self-employed IT professionals represent a notable example of combining the flexibility and autonomy of self-employment with high job satisfaction linked to survey responses such as "Autonomy in the way I carry out the job."

Another case in the IT context is that of AI-enabled autocomplete in programming environments, which is often extolled for its ability to adapt to "personal coding style" (Code Faster with AI, n.d.; Dechalert, 2020). This supports our thesis that artisanal style may survive and even be supported by digital automation. But that does not mean they are immune to low pay and other kinds of exploitation (Irani & Silberman, 2016). And even if that can be resolved in the case of software artisans, we should strive for technosocial design that can support artisanal economies in all sectors: whole ecosystems of meaningful and sustainable production and consumption in which networks of minimal extraction and maximized circulation can provide a more just and sustainable way of life (Eglash et al., 2020).

Much of the research into categories such as "craft" (Ratten et al., 2019) involves studies of artisan relations to the local community's lifestyle, goals and social fabric. These often draw on Bourdieu (2011) in identifying an essential characteristic of entrepreneurial activity: converting cultural, social and symbolic capital into economic capital. Pret et al. (2016) found that such value transformations were more circular than linear for creative entrepreneurs. For example, studies of craft brewers demonstrate that in addition to giving back to their local community, they will band together with other local craft brewers, sharing brewing tips and recommending each other's establishments to their guests (Flanagan et al., 2017). Synthesizing this with the previous notes on the spectrum between design and craft, we can define "artisan entrepreneur" as *those autonomously and communally engaged in the productive transformations of value across the spectrum of design and craft, such that value extraction is minimized and value circulation maximized.*

Artisan entrepreneurs are typically not solely focused on enriching themselves by converting other forms into economic capital. Instead, they tend to collaborate with other artisans, even as they compete with them. The merger of these two terms, in the neologism "coopetition," is occasionally fetishized in the "secrets of business success" pop literature, but when done authentically it can be a profoundly egalitarian practice, sharing connections and knowledge (Drummond et al., 2018; Kuhn & Galloway, 2015) and lending material support to other businesses and even to competitors (Al-Dajani et al., 2015; Pret et al., 2016). In this manner, artisan entrepreneurs are known to band together, circulating and converting forms of capital as a strategy to reduce purchasing costs (Flanagan et al., 2017), strengthen their overall position (McAdam et al., 2014) and compete with bigger competitors (Kraus et al., 2018).

We can view these strategies as limited forms of counter-hegemonic resistance, but they can also be the starting point for more transformative visions in which the entire economy is reengineered for egalitarian, unalienated value circulation, referred to as a "generative economy" (Eglash, 2016; Eglash et al., 2020) or "commons-based peer production" (Bauwens & Pantazis, 2018). Experiments toward that vision include aspects of the gift economy such as open source, as well as barter, time banks, local currency and even ordinary monetary exchanges as long as they are structured in ways that best enable local flourishing. This includes circulations to nonhumans as well, since ecosystem sustainability is also part of artisanal coopetition (e.g., competing for harvests while cooperating in maintaining the commons, as noted by Ostrom [2008] and others; for example [Jenkins et al., 2022]).

## Artisanal Politics and Practices as a Basis for Counter-hegemonic AI

We want to avoid yet another universalizing manifesto for ethical principles of AI, which often have levels of abstraction so high that they afford self-serving reinterpretations (for example the number of military and corporation leaders who would claim that their AI is, in some sense, contributing to the "social good" is probably close to 100%). On the other hand, needs-based participatory design, in which ordinary citizens have some voice, is often predetermined by the constraints imposed by implicit assumptions. The turn toward asset-based participatory design and its variations as modes of solidarity-based and culture-based design (Harrington et al., 2019; Karusala et al., 2019; Kumar et al., 2019; Mhlambi, 2020; Pei & Nardi, 2019; Wong-Villacres et al., 2021) may be a better way to think about strategies for bringing in artisanal communities, histories and practices in computing for a more egalitarian, unalienated economy.

Our current research on the participation side is funded by a grant from the National Science Foundation, "Race, Gender and Class Equity in the Future of Work: Automation for the Artisanal Economy." At this point (end of the first year) we have recruited 16 artisans and initiated on-boarding for another four, with all but one from Detroit MI (close to our campus at UM-Ann Arbor). So far the group is 100% African American and 80% female. They were recruited mainly by snowball method, allowing us to take advantage of some preestablished networks and ensure that the kinds of counter-hegemonic practices and goals of interest were already shared to some extent. In some cases the networks extended beyond the Detroit borders, including one textile worker importing cloth from West Africa. The occupations/products (including new recruits currently on-boarding) are quite diverse and include urban farming, textiles, adornment, education, cosmetology, toys, furniture and solar energy.

We have organized our approach by scale—micro, meso- and macroeconomic—in each case investigating the same question, informed by both the participants and the broader history of artisans outlined earlier: how can artisanal counter-hegemonic identity inform the development and deployment of AI and other computing design in establishing an economic ecosystem, through prefigurative and democratic means, whereby automation and other computational features can facilitate unalienated value generation and its circular flow, rather than extraction?

At the microscale, "authenticity" is one of the critical features by which artisans have always marketed goods and practices, as noted already. Our Detroit participants noted the threats raised for this feature in the shift to online consumption. One of our pilot projects (Robinson et al., 2021) developed AI for distinguishing between hand-woven cloth and the factory-made fakes that threaten this artisanal tradition by cost cutting. While the first phase was simply a proof of concept (which works; it can now make the distinction with a single photo), the goal is ultimately to help reconnect artisans to consumers: in the case of real cloths, the aim is a future app, which will identify the origin and allow "value added" (for example a guest lecture by the weaver for a class, further purchases from a particular family or collective and so on). With our artisanal participants we have discussed more ideas along this line of server-based structures, intelligent buying agents and so on to connect to consumers and artisans in ways that are more meaningful and sustainable. This is in keeping with the recommendations by Mhlambi (2020) that AI be used to shift us to a relational economy based on African Ubuntu traditions.

Other microscale practices, focused more directly on the Detroit group, involved the use of AI to generate a synthesis between traditional and nontraditional designs for textiles. Additional digital technologies such as laser cutting, 3D printing, soil sensing and digital measurement tools have also been deployed by participants, and we aim to investigate the ways in which they can be empowered by AI as well. These amendments might include the means of increasing productivity, variety, quality, sustainability, appeal to consumers and so on. On the one hand, this may sound no different than what any other producer looks for in new technologies. But thinking back to the Jura watchmakers, it is clear that innovation can be guided in ways that are particularly suitable to artisanal preferences. For example, the Jura desire to avoid factory work, and maintain home production, was the rationale for decisions about which technologies to accept or reject, and we have similarly worked on aligning innovation with our participants' preferences. A key feature we have uncovered in this process is the need to provide non-digital resources. These ranged from felt-pressing machines (prior to laser cutting) to heat sealers (for bags prior to digital labeling) to solar photovoltaics (to power sensing systems in urban farms).

At the meso-level, we encounter the link between enterprises. We are constantly bombarded by well-meaning advice about how we need to subcontract components to online customization companies, services and so on. Instead our artisans (and the history of their political struggles) suggest that horizontal links between enterprises and digital services such as e-fulfillment also need to be located in grassroots ownership. Additional ideas discussed include digital financing structures for pooling funds for group purchasing or mutual aid, intelligent agents to facilitate artisan to artisan supply chains, and new kinds of search engines that would better guide consumption practices toward the artisanal economy. A variety of strategies by which AI and associated technologies might facilitate such networks at both the meso and macro level for artisanal economies are further discussed elsewhere (Eglash et al., 2020); we look forward to reporting on their deployment and evaluation in the future.

## Conclusion

Scholars have emphasized the importance of examining algorithms and data to uncover bias and establish fairness standards. Despite its necessity, this "bias" framework is insufficient to achieve transformational improvements. This chapter argues that economic practices and political movements that artisans have offered, past and present, can provide principles, proof-of-concept demonstrations and communities of practice for how technological innovation might empower a grassroots economy, with the caveat that such transformation has always required political and social change as well. In particular, we find that new innovative strategies with technological advancements in artificial intelligence, robotics and other forms of automation can be formulated, deployed and investigated in researcher-practitioner partnerships of the kind we outline here with the goal of transformation to a more-liberated and less-alienated economic democratization.

**Acknowledgment:** The authors would like to acknowledge support from NSF award 2128756.

## References

Acemoglu, D., & Restrepo, P. (2019). Automation and new tasks: How technology displaces and reinstates labor. *Journal of Economic Perspectives*, *33*(2), 3–30. https://doi.org/10.1257/jep.33.2.3

Acemoglu, D., & Restrepo, P. (2020). Robots and jobs: Evidence from US labor markets. *Journal of Political Economy*, *128*(6), 2188–2244.

Al-Dajani, H., Carter, S., Shaw, E., & Marlow, S. (2015). Entrepreneurship among the displaced and dispossessed: Exploring the limits of emancipatory entrepreneuring. *British Journal of Management*, *26*(4), 713–730.

Baumol, W. J. (1993). Formal entrepreneurship theory in economics: Existence and bounds. *Journal of Business Venturing*, *8*(3), 197–210.

Bauwens, M., & Pantazis, A. (2018). The ecosystem of commons-based peer production and its transformative dynamics. *The Sociological Review*, *66*(2), 302–319.

Bourdieu, P. (2011). The forms of capital (1986). *Cultural Theory: An Anthology*, *1*, 81–93.

Brock Jr, A. (2020). *Distributed Blackness: African American Cybercultures* (Vol. 9). NYU Press.

Burawoy, M. (1990). *The politics of production*. Verso.

The Butchers Guild. (n.d.). Our mission. *The Butchers Guild*. Retrieved May 3, 2022, from www.thebutchersguild.org/about-the-guild-2

Carroll, G. R., & Wheaton, D. R. (2009). The organizational construction of authenticity: An examination of contemporary food and dining in the US. *Research in Organizational Behavior*, *29*, 255–282.

Cirillo, D., Catuara-Solarz, S., Morey, C., Guney, E., Subirats, L., Mellino, S., Gigante, A., Valencia, A., Rementeria, M. J., Chadha, A. S., & others. (2020). Sex and gender differences and biases in artificial intelligence for biomedicine and healthcare. *NPJ Digital Medicine*, *3*(1), 1–11.

Cleaver, H. (1994). Kropotkin, self-valorization, and the crisis of Marxism. *Anarchist Studies*, *2*(2), 119–135.

Code Faster with AI. (n.d.). *Code faster with AI code completions*. Retrieved May 9, 2022, from www.tabnine.com/get

Cope, Z. (2013). Global wage scaling and left ideology: A critique of Charles post on the "labour aristocracy." In *Contradictions: Finance, greed, and labor unequally paid*. Emerald Group Publishing Limited.

Costanza-Chock, S. (2020). *Design justice: Community-led practices to build the worlds we need*. The MIT Press.

Dechalert, A. (2020, April 1). What autocomplete can do for your productivity. *The Official Tabnine Blog*. www.tabnine.com/blog/autocomplete-productivity/

Drummond, C., McGrath, H., & O'Toole, T. (2018). The impact of social media on resource mobilisation in entrepreneurial firms. *Industrial Marketing Management*, *70*, 68–89.

Eglash, R. (2016). An introduction to generative justice. *Teknokultura*, *13*(2), 369–404.

Eglash, R. (2018). A generative perspective on engineering: Why the destructive force of artifacts is immune to politics. In E. Subrahmanian, T. Odumosu, & J. Y. Tsao (Eds.), *Engineering a better future: Interplay between engineering, social sciences, and innovation* (pp. 75–88). Springer International Publishing. https://doi.org/10.1007/978-3-319-91134-2_9

Eglash, R., Bennett, A., Cooke, L., Babbitt, W., & Lachney, M. (2021). Counter-hegemonic computing: Toward computer science education for value generation and emancipation. *ACM Transactions on Computing Education (TOCE)*, *21*(4), 1–30.

Eglash, R., & Foster, E. K. (2017). On the politics of generative justice: African traditions and maker communities. *What Do Science, Technology, and Innovation Mean from Africa*, 117–135.

Eglash, R., Robert, L., Bennett, A., Robinson, K. P., Lachney, M., & Babbitt, W. (2020). Automation for the artisanal economy: Enhancing the economic and environmental sustainability of crafting professions with human—machine collaboration. *Ai & Society*, *35*(3), 595–609.

Ehmer, J. (2001). Artisans and guilds, history of. In N. J. Smelser & P. B. Baltes (Eds.), *International encyclopedia of the social & behavioral sciences* (pp. 816–821). Pergamon. https://doi.org/10.1016/B0-08-043076-7/02706-6

Elkington, J. (2018, June 25). 25 Years ago i coined the phrase "triple bottom line": Here's why it's time to rethink it. *Harvard Business Review*. https://hbr.org/2018/06/25-years-ago-i-coined-the-phrase-triple-bottom-line-heres-why-im-giving-up-on-it

Flanagan, D. J., Lepisto, D. A., & Ofstein, L. F. (2018). Coopetition among nascent craft breweries: a value chain analysis, *Journal of Small Business and Enterprise Development*, *25*(1), pp. 2–16. https://doi.org/10.1108/JSBED-05-2017-0173

Friedman, T. L. (2010, October 24). The election that wasn't: Op-ed. *New York Times, Global Newsstream*. www.proquest.com/newspapers/election-that-wasnt/docview/759670566/se-2

Fuchs, C. (2014). *Digital labour and Karl Marx*. Routledge.

Gartner, W. B. (1990). What are we talking about when we talk about entrepreneurship? *Journal of Business Venturing*, *5*(1), 15–28.

Greiner, L. E. (1998). Evolution and revolution as organizations grow. *Harvard Business Review*, *76*(3), 55–64.

Grossman, G. M., & Oberfield, E. (2021). *The elusive explanation for the declining labor share*. National Bureau of Economic Research.

Hanagan, M. (1977). Artisan and skilled worker: The problem of definition. *International Labor and Working-Class History*, *12*, 28–31. Cambridge Core. https://doi.org/10.1017/S0147547900015441

Harrington, C., Erete, S., & Piper, A. M. (2019). Deconstructing community-based collaborative design: Towards more equitable participatory design engagements. *Proceedings of the ACM on Human-Computer Interaction*, *3*(CSCW). https://doi.org/10.1145/3359318

Hobsbawm, E. J. (1984). Artisan or labour aristocrat? *Economic History Review*, 355–372.

Hughes, T. P. (1994). Technological momentum. In *Does technology drive history*. MIT Press.

Irani, L. C., & Silberman, M. S. (2016). Stories we tell about labor: Turkopticon and the trouble with "design." *Proceedings of the 2016 CHI Conference on Human Factors in Computing Systems*, 4573–4586.

Jang, S., & Nam, K. (2022). Utilization of speculative design for designing human-AI interactions. *Archives of Design Research*, *35*(2).

Jenkins, M. E., Simmons, R., Lofthouse, J., & Edwards, E. (2022). *The environmental optimism of Elinor Ostrom*. The Center for Growth and Opportunity.

Kapur, S. (2021). Reducing racial bias in AI models for clinical use requires a top-down intervention. *Nature Machine Intelligence*, *3*(6), 460–460.

Karusala, N., Holeman, I., & Anderson, R. (2019). Engaging identity, assets, and constraints in designing for resilience. *Proceedings of the ACM on Human-Computer Interaction*, *3*(CSCW), 1–23.

Katz, L. (2014, July 15). Get a liberal arts B.A., not a business B.A., for the coming artisan economy. *PBS NewsHour*. www.pbs.org/newshour/nation/get-a-liberal-arts-b-a-not-a-business-b-a-for-the-coming-artisan-economy

Kneese, T., Rosenblat, A., & Boyd, D. (2014). *Technologically mediated artisanal production*. Open Society Foundations' Future of Work Commissioned Research Papers.

Knight, F. H. (1921). *Risk, uncertainty and profit* (Vol. 31). Houghton Mifflin.

Kraus, S., Klimas, P., Gast, J., & Stephan, T. (2018). Sleeping with competitors: Forms, antecedents and outcomes of coopetition of small and medium-sized craft beer breweries. *International Journal of Entrepreneurial Behavior & Research*, *25*(1), 50–66.

Kropotkin, P. (1899). *Memoirs of a revolutionist*. https://en.wikipedia.org/wiki/Memoirs_of_a_Revolutionist

Krugh, M. (2014). Joy in labour: The politicization of craft from the arts and crafts movement to etsy. *Canadian Review of American Studies*, *44*(2), 281–301.

Kuhn, K. M., & Galloway, T. L. (2015). With a little help from my competitors: Peer networking among artisan entrepreneurs. *Entrepreneurship Theory and Practice, 39*(3), 571–600.

Kumar, N., Sturm, C., Ahmed, S. I., Karusala, N., Wong-Villacres, M., Morales, L., Orji, R., Dye, M., Ahmed, N., Gaytán-Lugo, L. S., Vashistha, A., Nemer, D., Heimerl, K., & Dray, S. (2019). HCI across borders and intersections. *Extended Abstracts of the 2019 CHI Conference on Human Factors in Computing Systems*, 1–8. https://doi.org/10.1145/3290607.3299004

Landes, D. S. (1984). Revolution in time: Clocks and the making of the modern world. In *Revolution in time: Clocks and the making of the modern world.* Harvard University Press.

Leach, D. K. (2013). *"Prefigurative politics," the Wiley Blackwell encyclopedia of social and political movements.* Wiley Blackwell.

Lindley, S., Raval, N., Alavi, H. S., Lindtner, S., & Wang, D. (2019). The future of work. *Extended Abstracts of the 2019 CHI Conference on Human Factors in Computing Systems*, 1–8. https://doi.org/10.1145/3290607.3299008

Luckman, S. (2015). *Craft and the creative economy.* Springer.

Luckman, S. (2018). Craft entrepreneurialism and sustainable scale: Resistance to and disavowal of the creative industries as champions of capitalist growth. *Cultural Trends, 27*(5), 313–326. https://doi.org/10.1080/09548963.2018.1534574

Luckman, S., & Andrew, J. (2020). *Craftspeople and designer makers in the contemporary creative economy.* Springer Nature.

Manton, C., & Aga, B. (2021). *Conversational AI (technology that talks) and speculative design activism (2018–2019) [REF2021 collection].* http://researchspace.bathspa.ac.uk/13632/

Mazurski, K. R. (1991). Communism and the environment. *Forum for Applied Research and Public Policy, 5*, 39–44.

McAdam, M., McAdam, R., Dunn, A., & McCall, C. (2014). Development of small and medium-sized enterprise horizontal innovation networks: UK agri-food sector study. *International Small Business Journal, 32*(7), 830–853.

McMeel, D. (2021). Artisan to automation: Value and craft in the 21st century. *Architecture and Culture, 9*(4), 674–689. https://doi.org/10.1080/20507828.2021.1919854

McRobbie, A. (2018). *Be creative: Making a living in the new culture industries.* John Wiley & Sons.

Mhlambi, S. (2020). *From rationality to relationality: Ubuntu as an ethical and human rights framework for artificial intelligence governance* [Discussion Paper Series, 9]. Carr Center for Human Rights Policy.

Munck, B. D. (2019). Artisans as knowledge workers: Craft and creativity in a long term perspective. *Geoforum*, 99, 227–237. https://doi.org/10.1016/j.geoforum.2018.05.025

Nature Editorial Board. (2020). Africa's people must be able to write their own genomics agenda. *Nature, 586*(7831), 644. https://doi.org/10.1038/d41586-020-03028-3

Noble, D. F. (1978). Social choice in machine design: The case of automatically controlled machine tools, and a challenge for labor. *Politics & Society, 8*(3–4), 313–347.

Ostrom, E. (2008). Tragedy of the commons. *The New Palgrave Dictionary of Economics, 2.*

Oved, Y. (1992). The future society according to Kropotkin. *Cahiers Du Monde Russe et Soviétique*, 303–320.

Pei, L., & Nardi, B. (2019). We did it right, but it was still wrong: Toward assets-based design. *Extended Abstracts of the 2019 CHI Conference on Human Factors in Computing Systems*, 1–11.

Pennisi, E. (2021, February 4). Africans begin to take the reins of research into their own genomes. *Science*. www.science.org/content/article/africans-begin-take-reins-research-their-own-genomes

Pickering, A. (1995). *The mangle of practice: Time, agency, and science*. University of Chicago Press.

Piore, M. J., & Sabel, C. F. (1984). *The second industrial divide: possibilities for prosperity*. New York, NY: Basic Books.

Post, C. (2010). Exploring working-class consciousness: A critique of the theory of the "labour-aristocracy." *Historical Materialism, 18*(4), 3–38.

Pret, T., & Cogan, A. (2019). Artisan entrepreneurship: A systematic literature review and research agenda. *International Journal of Entrepreneurial Behavior & Research, 25*(4), 592–614. https://doi.org/10.1108/IJEBR-03-2018-0178

Pret, T., Shaw, E., & Drakopoulou Dodd, S. (2016). Painting the full picture: The conversion of economic, cultural, social and symbolic capital. *International Small Business Journal, 34*(8), 1004–1027.

Ratten, V., Costa, C., & Bogers, M. (2019). Artisan, cultural and tourism entrepreneurship. *International Journal of Entrepreneurial Behavior & Research, 25*(4), 582–591. https://doi.org/10.1108/IJEBR-05-2018-0319

Robinson, K. P., Eglash, R., Bennett, A., Nandakumar, S., & Robert, L. (2021). Authente-Kente: Enabling authentication for artisanal economies with deep learning. *AI & Society, 36*(1), 369–379.

Rule, J. (1987). The property of skill in the period of manufacture. *The Historical Meanings of Work, 107*.

SBA Profiles. (2018). 2018 Small Business Profiles for the States and Territories. The U.S. Small Business Administration. SBA.gov. https://www.sba.gov/advocacy/2018-small-business-profiles-states-and-territories

Schön, D. A. (1992). Designing as reflective conversation with the materials of a design situation. *Knowledge-Based Systems, 5*(1), 3–14. https://doi.org/10.1016/0950-7051(92)90020-G

Sennett, R. (2008). *The craftsman*. Yale University Press.

Sennett, R. (2020). Patterns and types of work in the past: Part 2. In *Work in the future* (pp. 33–36). Springer.

Simeone, L., Mantelli, R., & Adamo, A. (2022). *Pushing divergence and promoting convergence in a speculative design process: Considerations on the role of AI as a co-creation partner*. Proceedings of the DRS2022 Conference. https://doi.org/10.21606/Drs

Sirois, G. (2020). Artisan or designer. *Craft Entrepreneurship, 89*.

Solomon, S. J., & Mathias, B. D. (2020). The artisans' dilemma: Artisan entrepreneurship and the challenge of firm growth. *Journal of Business Venturing, 35*(5), 106044.

Sosteric, M. (2018, March 18). How money is destroying the world. *The Conversation*. http://theconversation.com/how-money-is-destroying-the-world-96517

Tanenbaum, L. (2014, December 1). My Brooklyn, not yours. *Jacobin*. https://jacobinmag.com/2014/01/my-brooklyn-not-yours

Tregear, A. (2005). Lifestyle, growth, or community involvement? The balance of goals of UK artisan food producers. *Entrepreneurship & Regional Development, 17*(1), 1–15.

Tremblay, D.-G., & Genin, É. (2008). Permeability between work and non-work: The case of self-employed IT workers. *Canadian Journal of Communication, 33*(4).

Veinot, T. C., Mitchell, H., & Ancker, J. S. (2018). Good intentions are not enough: How informatics interventions can worsen inequality. *Journal of the American Medical Informatics Association*, *25*(8), 1080–1088. https://doi.org/10.1093/jamia/ocy052

Vuilleumier, M. (2018). The first international in Switzerland: A few observations. In *"Arise ye wretched of the earth": The first international in a global perspective* (pp. 165–180). Brill.

Wasielewski, A. (2018). *Made in Brooklyn: Artists, hipsters, makers, and gentrification*. John Hunt Publishing.

Wong-Villacres, M., Gautam, A., Tatar, D., & DiSalvo, B. (2021). Reflections on assets-based design: A journey towards a collective of assets-based thinkers. *Proceedings of the ACM on Human-Computer Interaction*, *5*(CSCW2), 1–32. https://doi.org/10/gnk2sx

Wood, A., & Lehdonvirta, V. (2021). *Platform Precarity: Surviving algorithmic insecurity in the gig economy*. SSRN. https://papers.ssrn.com/sol3/Delivery.cfm?abstractid=3795375

Zietlow, R. E. (2020). The new peonage: Liberty and precarity for workers in the gig economy. *Wake Forest Law Review*, *55*, 1087.

# Index

AARon (rule-based system) 19
activity, domain 11
Adorno, Theodor 68
ad-supported subscriptions, launch 67
*Aeolian Silo* (Monahan) 29
African Ubuntu traditions, basis 82
AI on Return 0 20
Akten, Memo 20
algorithmic decision-making 46–47
algorithmic discovery system 46
algorithmic extraction 78
algorithmic intervention 49
algorithmic processes 36
algorithmic recommendation: power 61; system, claims 63
algorithmic turn 37
algorithms: mythology 67–69; potential 37–38; reliance 67; usage 55, 58–63
algo-torial logics 40–41
alienation, technologies 72
Amazon Mechanical Turk 80
Anadol, Refik 20
Arca 20
Aristotle 1, 23
art: AI developments, application 18–21; cybernetic art, cybernetics (relationship) 26–28
artificial intelligence (AI) 37–38; bias, example 71; concept 3–5; cybernetic approach 18; definitions, imprecision/contest 38; development 79; development, application 18–21; ethics 15; limits 24–25; music AI, interest (reasons) 40–46; outside forces 38–40; system 12–13; takeover, theme 21–22; technique 30; technologies, avoidance 15; turn 38; usage 47–48, 82; utopia, vision (Kurzweil) 24
artisanal economies 83
artisanal identity: automation, opposition 77; importance 74; role 71
artisanal labor, industrial appropriation 78
artisanal politics/practices 81–83
artisanal (category), US Small Business Administration (relationship) 73
artisan entrepreneurs: counter-hegemonic identity 76; impact 75
artisan identity, digital technology (intersection) 79–81
artisans: focus 72; identity, counter-hegemonic entrepreneur (relationship) 74–76; presence 73–74, 77–78; term, usage 78
artists, asymmetry 42–43
art-making process, demystification 27
Asimov, Isaac 21
audio-identifying apps, usage 39–40
audiovisual capitalism, transformation narratives 55
audiovisual industries (transformation), uncertainty (question) 56–58
audiovisual media, payment 65
audiovisual production, concentration 58
authenticity, importance 82
automation: artisanal identity, opposition 77; design 71; history, artisans (presence) 77–79
autonomy 80; undermining 77
autopoiesis 26

Baker, Bonnie 69
Bandcamp (audio app) 40
Barat, Robbie 20
bare extractive minimum 43
Bayesian model, usage 22
BBC (TV content) 66
Beaman, Jeanne 26–27
Beer, Stafford 26
Bennett, Audrey 71
Ben-Tal, Oded 20
Betzler, Monika 3, 7, 11–12, 15
Big Data: analysis 61; analysis, articulation 62–63; usage 61
Black Metal 20
blacksmiths, perception 73
*Black Widow* (movie) 55
Blenheim Chalcot 47
blind-bidding 57
block-booking 57
blockbuster audiences, maximization 58
blockbusters ("new economy") 55; placement 58
*Book of Knowledge of Ingenious Mechanical Devices, The* 23
*Book of the Machine, The* (Butler) 21
Boolean logic 26
Boomer (robot): damage 2; solidarity/recognition 12; treatment 8
Bostrom, Nick 22, 24
bottom-up transformation 78
brainstorming 9
broadband, usage (homes percentage) 59–60
Brün, Herbert 28
Bryson, Joanna 15
business, technology (threat) 38–39
butchers, cohesion/support network (loss) 76
Butcher's Guild, The 76
Butler, Samuel 21

CAD design 79
Cage, John 27–28; experimental music definition 29
Cameron, James 22
Čapek, Josef 21
Čapek, Karel 1–2
capital, global domination 73
capitalism: positive feedback loop 75; socialist replacement 72
capitalist growth mentality 76
capital-labour hybrid 38
Carpenter, Julie 2
Carré, Benoît 20
*Cartridge Music* (Cage) 28
catalogue strategy 58
categorization 46; algorithmic intervention 49
celestial jukebox, impact 44
Chartmetric (analytic service) 42
Chief Executive Officers (CEOs), starification 60
Chinese Room problem 24–25
Chung, Sougwen 30
Church-Turing thesis 25
classification 41
cloud-based digital music subscriptions 42
Cloud Painter (Van Arman) 20
cognition model 26
colleagues: feedback 9; harassing/bullying, avoidance 10; performance-based/behavioral criteria 3; qualification 7
collegial solidarity/recognition 11–14
collegial values, realization 11–14
Collins, Steve 36
*Colloquy of Mobiles* (Pask) 27
Columbia (minor studio) 57
commercial viability, scalability reliance 45
commons-based peer production 81
community/localism, corporatism (contrast) 75
company rhetoric, vision 72
computer aided design (CAD) 79
computer aided manufacturer (CAM) 77
computer, mind (relationship) 25–26
consistency, meaning 10
Consumer (Data) Science, goal 62
consumers, movie deliveries 59–60
consumer technology, capabilities (increase) 45–46
content: brands, amassing 65; filtering 41; investment risks, reduction 66–67; standardization 69; triumph 61
coopetition (neologism) 80–81

Cope, David 19
Copyright Act 1790, purposes 39
Copyright Act 1909, impact 39
corrective feedback 27
counter-hegemonic AI 71; artisanal politics/practices, basis 81–83
counter-hegemonic entrepreneur, artisan identity (relationship) 74–76
counter-hegemonic identity 76; characteristics 78; success 72
counter-hegemonic practices 81–82
counter-hegemonic resistance, limited forms 81
co-workers, solidarity/recognition 13
craft, mass production (contrast) 75
craftsmanship 79
creative arts, artificial intelligence/machine learning techniques (cybernetic approach) 18
creative machine-human collaboration 18; foundations, problems 21–24; trends/directions 30–31
creator phase (music industry entry) 46
*Crown, The* (TV series) 62
cultural industries school (France) 57
cultural production: center 69; risk 57
*Culture and Human-Robot Interaction in Militarized Spaces* (Carpenter) 2
cybernetics, cybernetic art (relationship) 26–28
Cybernetic Serendipity 26, 27
Cybernetic Serendipity Music 28
cyberspace, discourses 68

Dainton, Roger 27
DALL-E 2, visual extensions 18
Danaher, John 5, 6, 9
data: analysis 46; collection/aggregation/analysis 47; expertise, Netflix usage 61; extraction 41; feeding 48; music, equivalence 41; points 43; raw material 41; socio-demographic data, usage 58
data-dependent systems 71
data-driven analysis 48
data-driven organization, operation 62
data-driven solutions 45
data-intense gatekeeping activity 40–41
data science 36
datasets 37
Deep Dream (Mordvintsev) 19–20
deep learning (DL) 18
De Graaf, Maartje 5
democracy, authoritarian attacks 75
Depardieu, Gérard 66
deregulation measures 58
desired outcomes/goals, achievement 9
deskilling, enhanced form 72
Dick, Philip K. 22
differentiable digital signal processing (DDSP), usage 19
digital audio workstations (DAWs), roles (performance) 39
digital commodity 43
digital compression protocols 43
digital glass ceiling 78
digital music, participation (increase) 45–46
*Digital Sublime, The* (Mosco) 68
digital technology: advances 76; artisan identity, intersection 79–81
digital world, data collection/aggregation/analysis 47
Disney: strike-bac 65; trajectories 65; transformation, defense 55–56
disruptions 58–61
distribution infrastructure 43
Ditum, Sarah 68
diversity strategy 66
*Dream House* (Zazeela) 29
Dreyfus, Hubert 24–25
*Dripsody* (Le Caine) 29
*Dune* (movie) 55

Echo Next (shows) (Spotify acquisition) 42
ecological disasters 75
economic policy, influence 72
eDonkey (peer-to-peer network) 44
efficiency, perfect model 38
e-fulfillment 823
Eglash, Ron 71
Ek, Daniel 44
El-Dabh, Halim 29
electronically trainable analog neural network (ETANN) 21

Elgammal, Ahmed 19–20
Ellison, Harlan 22
employment diversity, necessity 71
entrepreneurial activity, characteristic (identification) 80
entrepreneurship, artisanal approaches 75
Epagogix, creation 56
*Erewhon* (Butler) 21
"Especially for You" (Adorno) 69
experimental music: Cage definition 29; patterns 29; perspectives 28–30
experiments in musical intelligence (EMI) system 19

Faber, Joseph 23
Fabulous Talking Machine (Faber) 23
feedback/freeforward loops 26
feedback loop 79
filtering, algorithmic processes 46
Fintech 48
first run houses, control 57
Fjelland, Ragnar 25
flexible specialization 77
Flute Player (Vaucanson) 23
follower growth, usage 48
Forrest, A.R. 27
FORTRAN 28
France, cultural industries school 57
FranceTV (TV content) 66
Franke, Herbert 19

Gamble, Lee 20
GAN-type models 20
Garvin, Matthew 71
GauGAN2 (Nvidia) 18
Gaussian noise, addition 18
Generative Adversarial Network (GAN): architecture 18–19; usage 20
generative economy 81
gig economy 78
gig workers, stereotype 80
Gillespie, Dizzy 29
GitHub 20
Gnutella (peer-to-peer network) 44
Gomez-Uribe, Carlos A. 62
Good Old Fashioned AI (GOFAI) 19, 25
GPT 3 (language model) 18
grassroots ownership 83
growth, risk-taking/pursuit 74–75
Guzdial, Mark 71

hand-craftsmanship 79
Hastings, Reed 59–60
HBO (cable channel) 60
Hello World (Akten) 20
Herndon, Holly 20
Hero of Alexandria 23
high-bandwidth telephony 43
Hiller, Lejaren 19
Hipgnosis 47
Hixon Symposium on Cerebral Mechanisms and Behaviour 26
Holly+ (Herndon) 20
Horkheimer, Max 68
Horowitz, Anthony 62
*House of Cards* (TV series) 60–61, 63
Hughes, David 36
human actions, imitation 12
human friends/partners, inner lives (absence) 6
human-level AI, criticism 24–25
human-level creativity, outperformance 37
human-machine collaboration 27–28
human-robot friendship, possibility 5–6
human-robot interaction 6
human-robot workplace interactions, solidarity/recognition (realization) 11–14
human-robot work teams, context 2
Hunt, Neil 62

I AM AI (Southern) 20
Ibn al-Razzaz Al-Jazari, Ibn Ismail 23
Iger, Bob 65
*Illiac Suite* (Hiller/Issacson) 19, 28
IMPALA 45
Imposture Series (Klingemann) 20
independence, conglomeration (contrast) 75
independent artisanal entrepreneurship, opposite 78
inequality, increase 75
informal conversations, engagement (ability) 9
information theory (Shannon) 29
*Infraudibles* (Brün) 28

innovation, failure 62
institutional affiliation 11
Intel 80170NX neural processor, usage 21
intelligent behavior: imitation 4; simulation/replication 4
intelligent machines, trends/directions 30
intelligent thinking 4
International Alliance of Stage, Theater and Film Employees (IATSE), unions (negotiations) 55–56
interpersonal values 11
Issacson, Leonard 19
*It's Gonna Rain* (Reich) 29
iZotope, Neutron 3 Advanced 46

James, William 29
Johansson, Scarlett 55
joint work, values (honoring) 10
Jukebox (OpenAI) 19
Jura watchmakers, factory work (avoidance) 82

Kaspar (robot) 4
Kazaa (peer-to-peer network) 44
Keith, Sarah 36
King Mu, impact 22–23
Kitarō, Nishida 29
*kleine Warenproduktion* (small commodity production) 73
Klingemann, Mario 20
Koosha, Ash 20
Kropotkin, Peter 74
Kubrick, Stanley 22
Kurzweil, Ray 22, 24

labor: apartheid, creation 79; aristocracy 73; aristocracy, Marx critique 78; division, shifts 77; reinstatement 71–72; unalienated labor, survival strategies 73
LaMDA (Google language model) 10
language models, transformer-based architectures (usage) 18
lean platforms 43
Le Caine, Hugh 29
legitimation, discourses 67–68
Lem, Stanisław 22
Lewis, George E. 29, 30–31
liberated economy, automation (design) 71
*Liezi* (Daoist text) 22
*Lillehammer* (TV series) 63
LimeWire (peer-to-peer network) 44
Linton, David 24
listenership, limitations 48
Live Nation, impact 48
long short-term memory models (LSTMs), application 21
Löschke, Jörg 3, 7, 11–12, 15
"Loud&Clear" (Spotify) 44–45
Lucasfilm 65
Luddites, rise 24

Machine Hallucination (Anadol) 20
machine-human collaborators, performance 30
machine learning (ML): computing hardware, availability 19; models 28; processes, usage 47–48
machine learning (ML) techniques 30; cybernetic approach 18; incorporation 20
*Machines Who Think* (McCorduck) 21
MacKay, Donald M. 27
macroeconomic scale 82
Magis, Christophe 55
major studios, domination 57
Malina, Frank 27
Markov Chains, application 19
"Marseille" (TV series) 66
Marvel Entertainment 65
Marx, Karl 71, 73–74
Mason, Maughan S. 27
mass culture, products 68–69
mass product, idiocy 69
Masterman, Margaret 27
master-servant dynamic 23, 30
McCorduck, Pamela 21, 22
McCulloch, Warren 26
Mead, Margaret 26
meaningful work 4
mechanization 77
media: capitalism (transformation), algorithms (mythology) 67–69; horizons, limitation 68; sector, concentration 58; structural changes, prolongation 66–67

Mercuriadis, Mark 47
Mesker, Alex 36
mesoeconomic scale 82
*Metastasis* (Xenakis) 29
Metro-Goldwyn-Mayer, impact 55
Metzger, Gustav 27
microeconomic scale 82
MIDiA (research report) 46
MIDI files, usage 19
mind, computer (relationship) 25–26
minor studios 57
Misselhorn, Catrin 13
MMC (venture capital firm) 38
mobile devices 43
MoffetNathanson 63
Monahan, Gordon 29
Monk, Thelonious 29
Monogram (minor studio) 57
monotony, enhanced form 72
Mordvintsev, Alexander 19–20
Morgan Stanley 47
Morris, William 74
Mosco, Vincent 68
Mouse on Mars 20
music: AI, interest (reasons) 40–46; archive, discovery 44; categorization, algorithmic intervention 49; creation, algorithmic intervention 49; curation, algorithmic intervention 49; curation, platformization 40–41; data, equivalence 41; datafication 41–42; digital asset 42–43; disruption 46–47; ecosystem, sense 47; production, automation 37; redefining 37; start-ups, investments 47; streaming, economics (UK Parliamentary inquiry) 44
musical product value, change 44–45
Music Business Worldwide (AI articles) 36
music industry: AI interest increase 40; artificial intelligence, impact 36; technology developers, cross-pollination 39
*Musicolour* (Pask) 27
"Music's Smart Future" (report) 36
mutual help/support, providing 10

Nake, Frieder 19, 27
Napster: launch 44; moments 39
National Science Foundation 81
Netflix: content assets *64*; content assets, growth 63, 65; content, commissioning 66; content spending *64*; data-driven organization, operation 62; data expertise 61; disruption capacity 60, 62–63; emergence/consolidation 59; exponential growth, reliance 66–67; impact 55; paid subscribers *67*; recommender system, usage 62–63; retooling 60; rise 56; service, abandonment (prevention) 63; system, warning 68; trajectory 58–63, 65; viewer ratings, connection 61–62
Neural Synthesis N° 6–9 (Tudor) 21
Neutron 3 Advanced (iZotope) 46
new economy 59; start-ups 60
New Hollywood era 57–58
niche content, articulation 62–63
nonfinancial focus, profit maximization (contrast) 75
Nullsoft, Winamp player 44
Nyholm, Sven 1

*Omnia per Omnia* (Chung) 30
*On Automata-Making*, designs 23
oppositional identity: nonfinancial focus 76; sense 75
*Orange Is the New Black* (TV series) 60–61
overproduction 58

Paik, Nam June 27
paradigmatic robots 4
Paramount Case of 1948 57–58
Parker, Charlie 29
participation, rhetoric 69
Pask, Gordon 26
pattern recognition, impact 48
payola 45
Pay TV: offers 65–66; progressive rise 58; services 61
peer-to-peer networks, emergence 44
performance indicators 12
personal coding style, adaptation 80

personal flair, notion 79–80
personalization, impact 63
Perticoz, Lucien 59
Petrič, Špela 30
Philo of Byzantium 23
Pierce, J.R. 27
Pitts, Walter 26
Pixar Animation Studios 65
*PL'AI* (Petrič) 30
platforms, dependency (creation) 78
playlisting, usage 48
plugin instruments/effects, usage 39
*Pneumatics* (Hero of Alexandria) 23
political economy (history), artisans (presence) 73–74
*Politics* (Aristotle) 23
Porter Robinson, Kwame 71
Portraits of Imaginary People (Tyka) 20
positive feedback loop (capitalism) 75
postindustrial society, automation 77
precarity, enhanced form 72
product: elimination 69; maintenance 75–76; use-values 57
pseudo-individualization 69
"Pure Experience" concept (James) 29

quality content, articulation 62–63

"Race, Gender and Class Equity in the Future of Work" (National Science Foundation) 81
ranking 46
raw audio waveforms 19
Reaganism, impact 24
reciprocal synthesis 79
recognition, collegial values (realization) 11–14
recommendation: algorithmic systems 68; algorithms 66–67
recommender system, usage 62–63
recorded music, value ("public good" conception) 45
Reichardt, Jasia 26, 27
Reich, Steve 29
relational economy, African Ubuntu tradition basis 82
relational identity, description 75
Renzo, Adrian 36
Replika (chatbot) 9, 10
responsibility status/level 11
return on investment, risk-taking/pursuit 74–75
revenue-creating data, generation 47
Rhimes, Shonda 66
rights-holders, streaming services (catalogue licensing negotiations) 42
risk, coping 62
risk management strategies 58–59
RNCM PRiSM 30
Robert, Lionel 71
robot: concept 3–5; creation, avoidance 15; friend/romantic partner function, philosophical debates (lessons) 5–6; recognition, desire 13; work 1–2
robot, colleague function 1, 2, 6–11; arguments 5; decisions 8; discussion 14–16
"Robots Should Be Slaves" (Bryson) 15
Roddy, Stephen 18
Rossumovi Univerzální Roboti—Rossum's Universal Robots 21
*Rossum's Universal Robots* (Čapek) 1
Royalty Exchange (royalty trading site) 47
royalty rightsholders, benefits 47
rule-based system 19
*R.U.R.* (Čapek) 21
Ryland, Helen 8

*SAKI* (Pask) 27
Sarandos, Ted 60
Scorsese, Martin 66
Scott, Ridley 22
self-fulfilling prophecy 72
self-improving AI algorithms 22
self-observation, response 27
self-regulation 26
"serious music" 29
server-based structures 82
Shannon, Claude 27; information theory 29
Shazam (audio-identifying apps) 40
Shi, Yan 22–23
Signal to Noise Loops 31
skilled artisans, labor example 74

skills, production 79
SKYGGE project (Southern/Benoît) 20
Smids, Jilles 9
social disasters 75
social markers 72
socio-demographic data, usage 58
Sodatone (analytic service) 42, 43
software as a service (SaaS) products, existence 46
solidarity, collegial values (realization) 11
source data, abundance 62
Southern, Taryn 20
Spacey, Kevin 61
Splice, offer 45–46
Spotify (audio app) 40–41; label dependence 40–41; stream rate experimentation 45
Spotify Premium (rate) 44
*Squid Game* (TV series) 66
star-system era 57
start-up economy, intentional product 37
*Star Wars* (movie) 65
Sterne, Jonathan 40
Stockhausen, Karlheinz 27
*Stratégie* (Xenakis) 28
streaming: catalogues, digital music participation (increase) 45–46; maturation 48; oligopoly, emergence 40–41; performance 48; services, music (existence) 42; wars 60–61
streaming-dominated ecosystem, value creation/extraction 41
stream-ripping, practice 45
structuration 63–67
Sturm, Bob 20
StyleGAN3 (language model) 19
sub-amateur market 45–46
subscription video on demand (SVOD): algorithms 56; platforms 55; services, establishment 65–66; services, rise 59; subscriptions, sales 67
Suzuki, Daisetz 29
sweatshops, existence 73
syntagm, usage 67–68

T5 (language model) 18
tagging 41
Tambourine Player (Vaucanson) 23
Taylor, Geoff 36
technological developments, necessity 13–14
technological disruption, continuums 46–48
technological evolution 72
technological momentum 72
technological singularity, concept 22
technological systems, redesign 72
techno-mediated immortality 22
technosocial change 73
technosocial design, attempt 80
Tencent Music Entertainment Group 47
Tesla bot 1
Thatcherism, impact 24
Time Warner (HBO ownership) 60
Toffler, Alvin 22
Transfiguración (Hexorcismos) 20
transformation, narratives 55
transformer-based architectures, usage 18
triple bottom line 75
Tudor, David 21
Turing test 6, 9; passing 12, 25–26
Tyka, Mike 20

unalienated labor, survival strategies 73
uncertainty, question 56–58
Universal-International Republic (minor studio) 57
US music revenues, growth (RIAA report) 40

value: alienation 71; creation 43; extraction 41
Van Arman, Pindar 20
Variational Autoencoders (VAE), Magenta project development 19
vertically integrated entertainment conglomerates, film corporations (connection) 58
Villeneuve, Denis 55
Vinge, Vernor 22, 24
Voisey creations 46
Von Foerster, Heinz 26
von Neumann, John 22, 26

Voyager: development (Lewis) 30; expansion 30
VQGAN (language model) 19

Warner Music UK 47
WaveNet (OpenAI) 19
Warner Music Group 43
Wiener, Norbert 26
Winamp player (Nullsoft) 44
*Wire Recorder Piece* (El-Dabh) 29
Withey, Conrad 48
work: concept 3–5; content, type 11; meaningful work 4
workplace relationships 11
workplace robots 10
work-related interaction, adjustment 10
work-related values, sharing 10
Wright, Robin 61

Young, La Monte 29
Yukou, Lie 22–23

Zazeela, Marian 29
ZDF (TV content) 66
Zen Buddhism 29
Zinovieff, Peter 27, 28

For Product Safety Concerns and Information please contact our EU representative GPSR@taylorandfrancis.com
Taylor & Francis Verlag GmbH, Kaufingerstraße 24, 80331 München, Germany

www.ingramcontent.com/pod-product-compliance
Ingram Content Group UK Ltd.
Pitfield, Milton Keynes, MK11 3LW, UK
UKHW021057080625
459435UK00004B/39